Finding Aster

our Ethiopian adoption story

by

Dina McQueen

INKWATER PRESS

PORTLAND • OREGON
INKWATERPRESS.COM

Finding Aster—our Ethiopian adoption story is a work of creative nonfiction. Unless presented with an attached footnote, most names of people, agencies, and cities have been changed. The names of the author's family members are real, as are the places where they lived and visited.

Dina writes with candor of her hopes, fears and frustrations as she seeks adoptive motherhood. She describes her path in a way that is informative, even at times cautionary, to anyone who might be considering international adoption and adoption from Ethiopia specifically. On her way to motherhood, Dina learns firsthand of the realities of Ethiopia where an entire generation of parents has been decimated by AIDS, leaving thousands of children orphaned. Dina does find Aster, but the search has been transformative and Dina not only adopts a child, she embraces a cause. Her book is not just a story about adoption; it is a call to adoption.

—Kathryn Pope Olsen, Founder, AHOPE for Children

This is a story about a family's journey toward parenthood that is at once unique and universal. We've all heard of biological imperative; well, McQueen successfully presents the spiritual imperative that motivated her and her husband to search for their daughter, Aster. McQueen is a wonderful storyteller who pulls no punches in her detailing of the international adoption industry. Nor, does she hide her own flaws. She shares her pain as well as her wisdom.

—Holly MacArthur, Deputy Publisher, *Tin House Magazine.*

Finding Aster is an engrossing read. The book is heart-achingly personal. There were times as a man that I had no way to fully understand what Dina had experienced. But as a parent and fellow human, I understood everything she felt totally and viscerally. I admire Dina's courage to have persisted in adopting Aster and to have written about herself so courageously.

—Nat Sloane, Co-Founder of Impetus Trust, London

Dina is a shining example of getting in the trenches with unconditional love and acceptance to create families for children in the system. The research, the outreach, the waiting and constant introspection did not deter Dina and Brian from believing in the fulfillment of parenting through adoption. Dina shows respect for the process, learning about her daughter and her country, and making a commitment for a forever family in extraordinary ways. And, Aster's life will be fulfilling with Dina and Brian as her parents!

—Lynn Price, Founder and President Emeritus, Camp to Belong

Dina's openness and honesty provide important insights into the complexities of adoption. She does not sanitize the adoption process but gives the good the bad and the ugly of her adoption experience. *Finding Aster* will help many to prepare for the rigors and not just the rewards of the international adoption process.

—Ina Cook, adoption attorney and adoptive mother

Finding Aster is Dina McQueen's unvarnished and moving account of the events that led up to the adoption of her Ethiopian daughter. The author details her personal struggles as a young woman searching for love and acceptance, and how her life's journey led her to a guesthouse in Addis Ababa, Ethiopia—and her first meeting with the orphaned Aster. Having grown up in a family with six adopted children, I am well aware of the joys and trials adoption can bring—the reams of paperwork, the many months (even years) of waiting, the uncertainty and second-guessing. McQueen unstintingly recounts the doubts and frustrations she encountered as she maneuvered through the adoption process, as well as the elation she felt when her efforts were ultimately successful. *Finding Aster* should be required reading for anyone considering international adoption.

—Chris Billing, Director, *Lost Sparrow*

This is a story of devoted persistence in the company of frustration and hope. But mainly it is a story of love, the love between a woman and a man and their love for a very special, beautiful little girl. This story is a moving beginning. We anticipate a sequel!

—Ambassador Harvey Nelson and Professor Esta Defossard-Nelson

Finding Aster is an inspirational and important read for the many families preparing to deliver a child through Ethiopia. The pages are filled with a raw and beautiful honesty. Thank you!

—Michelle Madrid-Branch, author of *The Tummy Mummy, Adoption Means Love: Triumph of the Heart*, and the upcoming memoir, *Difficult to Place*. Michelle serves on the Board of The Heart Gallery NM Foundation.

Dina's sensitivity and openness is really heartfelt. She engages the reader in an inner journey of self discovery and love that culminates through love in "finding Aster."

—Michele Meiche, Ct.H.A., Ph.D, Conscious Media Host/Producer of Awakenings Radio

*This book is dedicated to my
beloved daughter, Aster.*

Child, give me your hand
That I may walk in the light
Of your faith in me

                           - Hannah Kahn

CONTENTS

ASTER

Child
You live in this world
In a country known
To me
By just its name
Ethiopia   Ethiopia
Born from a mother
A father
You may never have seen
Never owned understanding
Of who they were

Child
I think about you
Daughter of my daughter
Daughter of my son
You will be
When they bring you
Home
America   America

Love for you
Already blooms in me
Like red apple
That spreads its strength
On hillsides
To hold the earth down
In the rain
Love reaching you
Through the miracle
Of thoughts
That prepare the place
In my heart
For you   Aster
Dearest granddaughter
Beloved child

Wendy Wolff Blumberg
For my granddaughter, Aster
Spring 2008

ACKNOWLEDGMENTS

Without the support and guidance from my oldest brother, Dan, I would not have finished this book. Thank you, Dan, for encouraging me to go deeper when the writing was shallow, and come up for air when I went too far. Also I would like to acknowledge my brother for his on-call readiness to co-parent from afar during our first year of parenthood. From that first night in Addis Ababa when he took a frantic phone call, to emails and phone support back home—he gives our every parenting concern serious attention and never makes us feel foolish.

A round of applause to my parents, who have spent their entire adult lives loving their four children. The example they set challenges me to be a kinder and more patient mother. Thanks, Mom and Dad, for helping see this book to print. Your belief in me as a writer means the world. There's nothing like the unconditional love of a parent, and I strive to give this to Aster.

Thank you to my talented first editor Jennifer Lawler, who saw the blank spots in the puzzle that was my book and figured out where the pieces were and how they fit together. I could not have done it without you.

Thank you to my friend, Marissa, for your detailed read-through. You found some holes I could not see and asked me to tell more of my truth. Not always easy, but as you know, necessary.

The final printing of this book would not be in its present form without the efforts of Esta and Harvey Nelson. Brian, Aster and I met Esta in the Ethiopian Air lounge on our way home from Addis Ababa, where she quickly became our fairy godmother and Aster's "Grandmother by affection," watching over us until we passed through Customs in Washington, D.C. The suggestions that Esta and Harvey made after reading the pre-publication version of *Finding Aster* served to elevate the writing and structure of my work. I am deeply grateful to them both.

Huge gratitude to the team at Inkwater Press: Sean, Masha, Linda, Kim and Rob—what a fantastic group of supportive people I had behind me. And what a great experience you all gave me. I cannot imagine a more helpful, intelligent group of people anywhere. Blessings to you all for helping me make the dream of *Finding Aster* come to fruition in such a satisfying way.

To my husband, Brian: we sure have come a long way together! Thank you for being my partner on this incredible journey of parenthood. There is no other man I would rather experience it with. I am so fortunate to have found you, and that you decided to take a chance on love with me. Most important, however, is that Aster has you to call you Daddy. Thank you for being here and being you, and always striving to be a more conscious human being. You inspire me to be a better mother. I love you.

FOREWORD

Let's face it: parenting isn't for everyone. Raising a child, at least a healthy, happy, well-adjusted one, is one of the most difficult and time-consuming jobs there is. Good parenting requires a commitment to learn and perform numerous skills that typically don't come very easily, especially when one's own parents were not particularly effective role models. Unfortunately, many, if not most, people don't think twice about these challenges. They procreate with ease, and pay little attention to their role in how their children turn out. This is, perhaps, the worst by-product of a society that grants unfettered reproductive rights, including to those who really have no business raising a child.

Theoretically, it is an entirely different story for those who struggle with fertility problems. These couples must continually reassess their reasons for wanting a child. The months, and often years, of medical interventions implemented to make a baby provide time to reflect on the couples' willingness to tackle the challenges of childrearing.

Likewise, most couples who choose adoption face the perils of parenting with their eyes wide open. Training is mandatory for these future parents. Moreover, these future parents are required to prove their suitability to state agencies tasked with overseeing that adopted children will be placed in "good" homes. (Shouldn't all children, adopted or otherwise, be afforded such protections?)

Despite all of the stress and hard work, raising a child can be supremely fulfilling. Just how rewarding the parenting experience will be, though, depends on the extent to which a couple focuses more on the child's needs than on their own. Ultimately, successful parenting is an exercise in self-sacrifice. Conversely, selfish parents are those who birth or adopt a child to fill a void in their life, to "save" their marriage, to make them happy, or to vicariously live through their children's successes. These parents fail their children on many levels.

Selfless parents come from the ranks of the adoptive and biological. However, it's not enough just to bring a child into this world or to rescue an orphan, despite your best intentions. The bottom line is that that child will not give your life meaning. Instead, effective parenting involves creating a physically and emotionally safe, cognitively challenging, nurturing environment in which the children are encouraged to reach their full potential—in whatever areas of interest and ability that they, and not their parents, choose.

In this book, you'll read the story of a couple who did not lightly approach the responsibility of parenting. When Dina was younger, she knew that she was not ready. But, when she was ready, it was too late to bring a baby into the world biologically. Undaunted and confident in the limitless love they had to give a child, Dina and her husband, Brian, pursued adoption. Their journey to conscious parenthood was a long, often emotionally difficult one. Her story describes the steps one goes through to accomplish an international adoption. But beyond that, Dina conveys the process they went through to embark on parenthood selflessly. These are lessons from which anyone who considers having a baby— biologically or through adoption—can benefit.

Daniel M. Blumberg, Ph.D.
Licensed Clinical Psychologist

PROLOGUE
WE BEGIN WITH THE END—
MEETING ASTER

I don't remember when the thin nanny in flip-flops holding the tiny baby entered the gated courtyard. She walked quietly towards my husband and me, and without saying a word, delivered my sleeping daughter into my arms. She turned and silently floated away like an angel returning to heaven.

It was 4:00 PM in Addis Ababa, Ethiopia. The images I now have in my mind were planted after the fact, thanks to a fellow adoptive mom who was sharing the guesthouse with us. She used our camera to document this magical moment on the first of five days spent in Africa.

It is, I suppose, a not uncommon journey. As with many women who long to have a child only to encounter a variety of obstacles, motherhood did not arrive quietly at my door. The voyage was filled with illness and disappointment, failures and near triumphs. But when finally it did knock, the event felt natural and awkward, surreal and yet lifetimes in the making.

This is the story of how we were united, a small vibrant Ethiopian orphan and me, a forty-six-year-old woman whose past ordeals now fade away in the light of my daughter Aster's joy.

CHAPTER ONE

MARRIAGE AT MID-LIFE

In looking back upon my youth, I do not recall ever having seriously contemplated motherhood. I don't know if this was a case of "nature" or "nurture," but it seems obvious now that I was not destined to go the traditional route; it was not in my cards to marry and have kids in the so-called conventional way.

On the heels of the sexual revolution of the 1960s, however, not getting married in your teens or early twenties didn't mean that a woman remained abstinent. My sexual urges became manifest at nineteen as a sophomore in college when I lost my virginity to a "bad boy" fraternity guy during my semesters at UCLA. This is where love and sex and career got all mixed up. I had little direction for a future, but it was obvious that this boyfriend would not end up being the forever man who would one day father my children.

By my fifth and final year in college, I realized that I had made a mistake in my choice of majors. Though I had declared a major in Fitness/Nutrition, during my senior year I was beyond bored and regretful. I gravitated toward Creative

Writing when completing the required electives, knowing there was no way I would go into the field of Corporate Fitness, where most of my fellow students were headed. Five days after graduation I left for Europe. I would be gone for five months with just a backpack, a Eurail pass, and a journal. It was 1985, and I was able to live, fairly extravagantly, on $10.00 a day. As money was not a concern, a newfound vitality emerged that allowed me to explore the outside world, as well as the world inside me. I felt no stress about the future, and for the first time since childhood I lived in the "now." The experience changed me. I realized with startling commitment that I wanted to be a writer, and would do what it took to make that happen.

During my twenties and thirties, I was a relatively healthy, relatively normal woman, and thus did not feel the need to avoid romance just to pursue a career. During these decades, though, I did feel conflicted between wanting to be in love (which did not mean, in my case, practicing *how* to love) and desiring to advance in the world of publishing. When I returned from Europe in November 1985 to Southern California, I immediately began to focus my creative energy on cultivating work in the publishing industry. It took less than one year to land my first job in my chosen field as the office manager/editorial assistant at a Santa Monica sports magazine. At night during the week and on weekend days I stayed in and nurtured my craft, writing short fiction. I was so focused on becoming a published writer that even though I dated here and there, I was not attracted to men who may have been interested in developing a long-term relationship.

In early fall of 1989, I accepted a job I had been pursuing as the production editor at a travel trade magazine in San Francisco. Though my real fantasy would have been to be in New York working for Condé Nast, moving to San Francisco was a good second best. I had been hired to do production, which was completely new to me, but I felt confident knowing that the managing editor believed I could handle the job. Then, at the end of my fifth day on the job, *The Big One* struck (a 7.1 earthquake), shaking up the city and shattering my personal sense of stability.

A few months into the job, though, as the city returned to some sense of normalcy, a daily rhythm took hold. I began to appreciate my good luck being able to live and work in San Francisco. I took on more responsibilities at the magazine and was assigned short promotional pieces. After two years, however, the job had run its course. I had mastered my duties and wanted to be moved into a position as staff writer. I was told in so many words that my wishes would never come true.

To fill in the loss of creativity I was feeling on the job, I began a self-study in screenwriting, which led to a desire to go to film school at San Francisco State University. After the first semester of night school, I became so obsessed with this program I gave my two-week notice. To save money, I moved from my Pacific Heights studio into a shared apartment with three undergraduate girls out near the university.

I loved studying film. Nearly everything about it. Except that after I completed my first film using a Super-8 camera and a manual splicing machine, I realized I actually did not want to make films; I was only interested in writing them.

When I spoke with the department head about this, he told me each student had to learn all aspects of filmmaking, and if I really wanted to concentrate only on screenwriting, I should get my butt to Hollywood.

Then, my decision was made for me. Blood appeared during a mid-cycle ovulation. I dropped out during my third semester, and underwent an abdominal surgical procedure called a laser laparoscopy, which determined that I had endometriosis. At the time, one of my cousins was a production coordinator on big budget commercials, and offered me a job with her L.A.–based company as a production assistant (P.A.), a.k.a. "go-fer." I accepted her offer and moved from my shared flat in San Francisco into a studio apartment in a rundown building in Santa Monica and spent nearly a year as a P.A. But that kind of work was not for me. I just couldn't do it.

So I signed on with a headhunter, who in 1993 found me what would soon turn out to be a too-good-to-be-true publishing job. I was the Executive Assistant for a small children's book publishing company in Beverly Hills. They paid me too much for too little work and promised me a lucrative and creative future. Sadly, just three months into it, the company went bankrupt and I was back on the street.

When I got laid off from the publishing job, I was living in a guesthouse on the less than opulent fringes of Beverly Hills. My brother Ron had just bought a beach cottage in San Diego that also had a guesthouse. He offered it to me for just $300 a month. I accepted, able easily to make rent on the unemployment checks and when that ran out, a part-time job at Starbucks. I enrolled in a novel-writing extension class at UCSD and structured my days around working on my first novel, taking only the night shifts at the coffee house. This is also when I met a man who two years later would manipulate me into having an abortion.

IN THE SPRING OF 1996, about sixteen months after the abortion, my parents took their four children and their families (I was the only single one at that time) to a dude ranch in Durango, Colorado, to celebrate their fortieth wedding anniversary. A week spent outdoors breathing mountain air, eating fresh foods, and hearing the silence that accompanies one at 7,000-feet elevation shrouded me in peace. I experienced a feeling of total oneness with the land upon which I sat. I fell in love with Durango, and like a woman who leaves her hometown to pursue the love of her life in some far-off destination, three months after returning from the dude ranch holiday, I left San Diego and moved to Durango.

As I was moving, I received a letter of acceptance into an off-campus graduate program at Vermont's Goddard College. In San Diego, I had facilitated journal-writing workshops in local bookstores. I found the work exhilarating, and knew that if I ever wanted to gain more legitimacy as a writer's coach or editor, I would need credentials. So I applied, and was accepted into the program, which I completed while living in Durango. It took three semesters to earn my master's degree in Biography/Autobiography, and in January 1998, I received my diploma.

The M.A. after my name did actually help further my career. While in graduate school, I had met various writers in Durango who wanted my help. After graduating I returned from Vermont with my piece of paper signed by the college president. I framed the diploma and hung it on the wall. Now I would be taken seriously. Gradually, I acquired clients and helped them write their stories. In 2000, I invested in desktop publishing software, as it was known then, and taught myself how to design and publish books. This was certainly the right career for me. I loved making books. And that was that.

Of course, during these years of focusing on my development as a writer/editor/publisher, I dated and even lived with one boyfriend for a year. But I was attracted to beautiful, athletically inclined men, and the relationships never led to anything long lasting. Because I seemed to be more interested in advancing my career than I was in developing a bond that would lead to a marriage, I got what I put out there: relative success at work, but failure at relationships. For fifteen years, I had pushed myself in the world of publishing, but I hadn't learned how to work at cultivating lasting connections with men. I realize and now accept that had I really wanted a dynamic, healthy relationship with a man, I would have put more energy into making that happen, even if I may not have known how.

However, since I did finally have satisfying work that I enjoyed and felt good about, I accepted being a single woman and decided to continue concentrating on publishing books. In 2002 I reluctantly admitted that no matter how much I liked living in Durango, if I wanted to make a living as a book editor and publisher, I would have to move. I chose Santa Fe, New Mexico, where my parents lived half the year. Santa Fe was filled with people who were eager to pay for the services of a writing coach, so this was a good choice. Word got out that I was committed to helping writers not get ripped off while self-publishing their books, and soon I had several projects that kept me busy. I maintained a well-rounded life by taking classes at a nearby yoga studio, and I lived close enough to town that I could walk or ride my bike most everywhere I needed to go. Life was pretty good. Even without a man in my life.

It was during this time that I began contemplating, albeit not very seriously, becoming a mother as a single woman. I wondered about adoption, and even questioned whether I would ever consider a sperm donor. These thoughts that were discussed over coffee with other 40-year-old single women, or contemplated at night while in bed with my cat sleeping close by, had originated while I was still living in Durango a year or so earlier. One winter afternoon, while fighting a bad flu bug, I caught the tail end of an *Oprah* show. All I remember about that particular "Aha!" moment is that Oprah looked into the camera and asked, "Okay, you're on your death bed and you're asked if you have any regrets. What's the first thing that pops into your mind?"

"I was never a mother."

I looked around my tiny, tidy living room filled with Pottery Barn furniture as if I were on *Candid Camera*: maybe someone was playing a joke? If my spontaneous outburst about not being a mom was true then I was in trouble. At the time, the relationship with the Durango live-in boyfriend had ended. I was thirty-eight years old, and didn't feel anywhere ready to pursue another intimate relationship.

Two years later, now living in Santa Fe, I wondered if I was capable of going through with an adoption or an insemination on my own. When I let the thought go far enough, it always came back to this: I didn't feel physically capable of working and raising a child, and I didn't have enough savings to go without an income.

IN JUST ANOTHER YEAR, THE spring of 2003, Brian came into my life. How? Well, first of all I was finally feeling successful in my career. With accolades from clients, and the satisfaction of seeing books that I made with my imprint on the spine, I could breathe an internal sigh of, *Ahhh*. I felt good about myself, which pop psychology confirms is a vital first step to finding and maintaining a solid relationship. My heart felt healed from the past, so I let myself think that maybe it was possible to find a man with whom I could explore a healthy partnership.

As the story goes, I had been secretly admiring my mailman since he had acquired my route, which was for about six months. Once in a while he came to the door with a package, but mostly I watched him from my living room window as he put the letters in the boxes at the end of the driveway. He had long sun-splashed hair that he wore pulled back in a ponytail, which I found really sexy. His pronounced facial features further attracted me, as well as his solid, slim build.

One noontime in May 2003, I acknowledged to myself that I was—yep—sexually attracted to him. I had just emailed the digital copy of a client's book to the Michigan printer. I was rushing to another client's house to help her sort out her poetry and I was late. But I had a stack of bills I needed to get out. At least that was the motivation I presented as I approached this letter carrier, who was pulled over at the side of the road. I felt nervous because he was so cute, and it had been a long time since I had felt these kinds of feelings. I didn't know if I was actually prepared to look him in the eyes, but I pulled up to his mail truck anyway and he came out as I handed him the letters. He seemed really excited too, especially when I asked him something that I now realize was a bit rude.

"I know you deliver the mail for a living, but what do you really do?"

"Hang on," he said and rushed to his truck. He trotted back and handed over a stack of photographs.

"I knew it," I said, somewhat smugly. "You're an artist."

The photos were of his large canvases that he painted late at night. Huge pieces of art, with incredible detail, color, and precision. One depicted two mermaids, their scales painted with such intricacy there was no doubt in my mind that his talent was strong enough to be represented in one of Santa Fe's finest galleries. I was wowed. And I can now admit, though I could not then, as I was too fearful of allowing my fantasy world to get the best of me, that this was the kind of man I had been looking for, well, perhaps forever. A guy with a solid job (which showed stability, something I did not exude myself), who was passionate about art and the making of it. He was obviously a man who had learned how to live in both worlds, committing to his craft, but not losing himself in the illusion that pursuing one's passion is enough to pay the bills.

Before driving off, we exchanged phone numbers. "By the way," he said, "my name is Brian. Brian Joseph McQueen." Of course he knew my name.

On the way to my client's house, I recognized that I felt something like, maybe ... lust? In the several days that passed before he called me, I allowed myself to feel desire, something I rarely permitted. I acknowledged that I wanted to get to know him. When he did call, and we spoke that first night for several hours, I knew for sure that I was prepared to follow my hunch and invest in trying to become a good partner. I was hoping that he would be too.

On September 5, 2004, at age forty-two, *I married the mailman*. The Santa Fe wedding at the city's historic La Fonda Hotel was my father's gift, not only an extravagant way of displaying his love for me, but also his way of letting everybody know how thrilled he was that I had finally found a wonderful man to marry.

Though part of my initial attraction to Brian was based on the fact that he was an artist who had a stable job with benefits, after we got involved I began to see that he really didn't enjoy the work as much as it had originally seemed. Often after work he would come over for supper then have to drive the forty-five minutes south where he lived with his two dogs. I told him fairly soon after we started dating that I wasn't up for us living together prior to being engaged—having done that and failed—and this boundary had its limits. He was now giving most of his free time to developing a relationship with me. There simply wasn't enough time in the day to do it all.

I saw his talent and his passion for painting and didn't want him to give that up. Of course I didn't want him to give me up either. Something, though, did have to go. I suggested that he quit his job and somehow we would make it work without his paycheck from the post office. My solution, in retrospect, could be seen as short-sighted and even selfish. Perhaps because I had been taking care of myself for nearly two decades, I was naïve and harbored romantic ideas about what our union would mean. I did not need him or his money to take care of me, and since we were in love I believed we would be okay. If he sold his house and moved in with me, with our combined savings we would be able to handle the bills until he was able to make a name in the art world. In a subtle way, it's obvious to me now that I was being manipulative. Even if I was not consciously aware, I think that I may have been twisting the situation in a way that he would have no choice but to ask me to marry him. Maybe urging him to quit his job was a way for me to feel in control of his destiny. Though I loathe to admit it, back then that was me.

Marry we did, however, and there I was forty-two and just embarking on a lifetime commitment to a man. It would take years before I learned how to compromise and love in a way that sustains a healthy marriage, years before I would learn to honor and respect the way things are rather than always trying to make it "better." Though we may not have admitted it, when we first decided to get married we both still had a lot of growing up to do. Four moves, four years, several near-divorce-experiences, and a major surgery is what it took for us to know for sure, without a doubt, that we were in this thing for good.

THROUGHOUT THE FIRST THREE YEARS of our marriage, Brian and I talked about having children. It was a romantic idea, more than a practical one, as we both were concerned about finances. Neither one of us felt strongly enough about making a baby together to send him back to a forty-hour-a-week job. Even though some people say that it doesn't cost that much to raise a child, the pregnancy alone would have been a strain, as my health insurance policy did not cover it, and with my medical history of endometriosis and related complications, I would never have risked a home birth. It was only later that my husband told me there had been an additional secret reason he didn't want us to become parents: he was worried about my health, and fearful that I would not be able to handle the stress and physical stamina it took to be a bio-mom.

Aside from fear over money and health, though, we were totally ambivalent about giving up our free time. We appreciated not having to be anywhere at any certain time, meaning if we wanted to stay up late working into the wee hours of the morning, that was okay. We could read what we wanted, when we wanted, eat late if the day dictated it, hop over to a neighbor's house spur-of-the-moment for a glass of wine, or skip dinner altogether and opt instead for popcorn and Dots in front of a rented movie. I could get a part-time job to supplement my work as an editor—or not. And he could spend ten months on a mural due to incessant rain instead of doing a half-assed rush job just to get through it in order to get to the next job. We did not live extravagant lives, and still don't, but if I wanted to buy a new winter coat, I would let myself.

During our time together while I was suffering from endometriosis, I was either on the pill or we used the rhythm method in order not to get pregnant. When a period was late, which often was the case, I secretly would imagine what it would feel like to be pregnant and give birth to a child I created with Brian. These short-lived fantasies I knew were normal; I accepted that I was a woman and with that comes at least a biological curiosity. I know now, though, that even if we had tried, it most likely would not have been successful. In retrospect I am glad that my urge to experience bio-motherhood with Brian wasn't strong; that desire probably would have ended up in disappointment.

However, there was more to our particular childless situation as a married couple. Whenever one of us seriously brought up the idea of me getting pregnant the topic of overpopulation would eventually arise. We did not feel good about adding another person to the planet. No matter how back-and-forth we may have been about creating a life from our DNA, we were never confused about how we felt about the environment. Every time we discussed making a baby, it stayed just that: romantic chitchat spoken from a place of fantasy. We just could not seem to get past the mental blocks we had set in place from day one around making and raising a baby, which included a planet suffering from overpopulation.

I understood then, and more fully realize now, that I live with a contradiction: regret and grief over having had an abortion, and encouraging others to adopt as a way to grow their family. I see the two, however, as separate entities. Unplanned pregnancies are epidemic today, and I do not advocate abortion. What I do support, and want others to commit to, is conscious discussion about making a baby. If I had gotten pregnant without Brian and me trying, I would have hopefully delivered a healthy baby. I know we would have accepted the miracle of life with gratitude. This does not mean that I am not concerned about the by-product of overpopulation, however, or that I will stop urging couples to consider adoption as a way to consciously create a family. (See Appendix A for a more extensive presentation on this topic.)

For us, though, as I continued to struggle with endometriosis, pregnancy rarely even seemed like a biological possibility. Despite decades of traditional medical and alternative treatment, I did not appear to be headed for bio-motherhood.

CHAPTER TWO

HYSTERECTOMY

*I*t's *not a bad idea at mid-life to hire a skilled physician to cut you open and peer inside. Remove what has grown defective. Like an archeological dig of sorts, excavating decayed parts. In two days, I will arrive at hospital mid-day on a full moon and admit myself for an elective hysterectomy that I agreed to two weeks ago. So, at 45, three years married and childless, I am heading into the third and final stage of life as a woman: wombless yet pregnant with possibility. Soon, with no more pain, no cyclic fatigue, ovarian cysts, cramps, or midnight nausea, the sky may surely be limitless. I have paid my dues and then some as a woman. Now, I am ready to see what's next.*

–Journal Excerpt 9/22/2007

THE HOSPITAL GOWN IS SHORT and flimsy. My frayed leg-warmers and old blue scarf try to keep me warm as I lie on a rolling bed in a refrigerated room segregated from the outside by a curtain. My seventy-five-year-old mother sits at my side, wrapped in a purple fleece poncho. She holds my icicle hand and offers her angel presence that decades of spiritual practice have cultivated. I am her only daughter of four children, a '60s child raised on civil rights marches and Hostess Twinkies. I am headed for the surgery of a lifetime, and too depleted from enforced fasting to worry. Mama smiles softly into my vacant eyes and affirms that finally, after thirty years of suffering "female troubles," I will soon be living pain-free.

For the past several years I had been a patient of a well-respected Santa Fe nurse practitioner who offered traditional women's health care, such as annuals and prenatal care, as well as homeopathy and other alternative modalities. This once-midwife was good to me when I came to her for help. She listened attentively and with compassion, and always supported my drive to be healthy. On several occasions, upon my request, she gave me prescriptions for ultrasounds in order to investigate the pelvic pain that I suffered. Nothing more than minor "functional" cysts ever showed up. Despite my chronic pain, she provided little genuine relief and even fewer recommendations for any sort of cure.

Come winter 2007, I no longer wanted to listen to the song we had been dancing to for, oh, about five years. I was no longer interested in describing what was going on, as she took copious notes in my file, *same old same old* ... I didn't want her to suggest more hormone creams, herbs, or vitamins. I was not willing to continue forking over $100 a visit knowing that in the end, nothing would change. My homeopathic nurse practitioner had turned out to be no different than all the past "traditional" physicians who struggled to make sense of this lingering and, to them, unexplainable, yet often excruciating pain I was in. Although she, like they, continued to take my money while offering suggestions for pain management, none had much interest in or patience for getting to the bottom of what was causing my misery. Eventually even the most caring provider would throw in the metaphorical towel and suggest I see a shrink. Doctors had often pushed psychotherapy and/or antidepressants on me—their way to deal with how depressed I'd become living with the pain and fatigue I'd suffered since my late twenties. "Maybe you would benefit from some therapy," they'd said, which always resulted in me doubting my own sense of knowing that something was quite wrong with my body.

So, the time had come, I felt, to go back to a licensed, board-certified, fully qualified M.D. who was as committed as I was to finally, once and for all, getting to the bottom of things. Possessing a lousy track record with health providers, at least when it came to this terrible pain, and no one to turn to for a referral, I did what any desperate person would do: I went to the Yellow Pages to find a new doctor.

Picking a doctor from a list of advertisements isn't difficult. There were not many women ob/gyn doctors, and I wanted a woman, so this narrowed my options. There is no rational reason why I chose the doctor I did. I picked one that had paid for a color ad, and I went to her website. She seemed bright, busy, and her eyes looked kind. A short explanation of the services her practice offered helped me pick up the phone and make an appointment.

During our initial meeting, Dr. Lowe assessed me and decided it might be a good idea to check out my pelvic pain with an ultrasound, which I thought was fine because she had to start somewhere. I knew if it were some kind of cancer causing the pain across my left abdomen that this would help her decide what to do next. I felt safe knowing that if, indeed, something was found, at least she was also a surgeon and she would know what to do and be able to do it herself.

The test results were read by the radiologist and revealed that an ovarian cyst on my left ovary had burst, and the fluid was floating around inside of me. Dr. Lowe believed this is what was causing the nausea and fatigue. It would take some time, but she assured me the fluid would eventually disappear.

Months passed, and I was still suffering. During our initial visit, of course I shared my medical history with Dr. Lowe, which included the laser surgery some fifteen years earlier. I also shared with her that after years of taking various kinds of birth control pills to halt having a menstrual cycle, and having tried everything from bio-identical creams to hypnotherapy, I believed the endometriosis was still running amuck throughout my system. I complained to her that for years now my entire life had revolved around efforts to relieve my suffering. Looking back, I had a lot of compassion for myself. I had no idea how serious my condition was, and I was trying really hard to avoid what most people in my life would eventually try to talk me out of. For years I had joked, "I wish I could just have it all taken out." I now realize that it was no joke.

Six months after I met Dr. Lowe, the burst cyst had dissolved and along with it, the constant abdominal pain. But, I still was suffering strange symptoms. Though I knew there was nothing else left for my doctor to offer except a hysterectomy, and I couldn't imagine going that route, I kept an appointment I had made a month earlier.

"I don't know why I'm here," I said. "Nothing has changed."

Her serious gaze convinced me that she did want to help. She explained that with my history of endometriosis, it is possible that the endometrial tissue had adhered to my bladder, my intestines, possibly even my lungs.

"Please," she pleaded with me, "let me help you."

Why hadn't a single person among the merry-go-round of health providers I had consulted over the years ever explained this to me? Finally, someone said something that not only made sense, but also gave me some hope.

I started to cry then, because I knew exactly what she meant, even though my tears also may have been a sign of relief that maybe, just maybe, this would all be over soon. She knew that I didn't have children. I asked her if it was true that if I went through a pregnancy, the endometriosis would go away.

"Perhaps," she told me.

But in my condition, and at my age, the likelihood of getting pregnant was slim to none. (For more information on infertility, see Appendix B.) And even if I did manage to get pregnant, after I gave birth the endometriosis would most likely grow right back.

I sat curled into myself across from the mahogany desk that separated us. The phone rang. She ignored it and continued looking at me with a gentle smile that indicated to me how deeply concerned she was. I sat there thinking about how exhausted I had become. I thought and thought about what it would mean to be cut open and all that went along with such a major surgery. I also, though, thought about the relief that was sure to follow. I leaned forward with my elbows on my knees and took a deep breath.

"Okay," I finally said. "Let's do it."

I LET GO OF MY mother's hand while she recites the Unity Prayer of Protection. When the orderly comes to take me away in the middle of her prayer, I want to tell him to wait, but whatever they put in the IV has nearly knocked me out. I have already lost control of my voice, but my mind can still think, and I am thinking that I am not ready for this.

By the time I am being rolled out of the curtained cubicle I hear my mother's voice fade into black. The next thing I remember is this: *I am lying flat on my back. My limbs are frozen. I feel too blissful to even try to move. In my mind there is a sweet voice that repeats the Medicine Buddha mantra, a healing prayer recited in Sanskrit.*

The last song I remember hearing on the CD that played through the headphones that the anesthesiologist had attached to my ears was Deva Premal singing the Medicine Buddha mantra. My eyes remain closed, and my body feels perfect. My mind sings the mantra and I feel a smile spread across my face, though I know I have had enough anesthesia to trick me into only thinking I am smiling. I am vaguely aware of hospital staff scurrying about me, only slightly cognizant that I am being wheeled someplace. It feels like a carnival ride, like I've swallowed something forbidden and the veil between what matters (my bliss) and what is true (this drug is going to wear off sooner or later, so you might as well enjoy it while you can) is about to be shredded.

As I very slowly leave the delightful oblivion of anesthesia, I am conscious of being rolled out of the room in which I had been resting. I know there is an IV in my vein, and I must have a morphine drip, as I am unable to even lift my arm. When I open my eyes I notice the room in which I have landed looks like a hospital scene out of a B-movie from the 1950s. I need to wipe a tear that rolls down my cheek because I am really disappointed, but I cannot move, not even a little bit. I want all of the anesthesia back in my blood so I don't have to face what lies ahead.

Looking back I am astonished that my first thought was not, *Wow, I didn't die on the operating table!* All I noticed, and I feel foolish admitting this, was that I had been given the ugliest hospital room in the country. What a shock this was considering when I checked in for my surgery earlier that day, I was in the recently remodeled section of the hospital, with overstuffed chairs in Southwest color schemes and framed art on the walls, all the trappings of a modern hospital. The only part of the hospital that had not been refurbished was the post-operative obstetrics ward.

My parents are here, and my husband. And flowers, beautiful flowers. Fearful but relieved expressions show on my family's faces. I hadn't died on the operating table, and I know they are pleased. But I feel completely knocked out still and I wonder why they have brought me to my room in this state. My husband has never seen me in such a vulnerable position. I was worried that he might be freaking out inside and trying not to show it. I wanted the bliss back, because I did not have the strength to take care of anybody else's anxiety.

"The doctor said that the surgery went very well," my mother begins. "You were her first 'non-bleeding' hysterectomy."

I'm not sure what this means but I'm too out of it to ask. Mom explains that it had taken about an hour, is all, to remove the uterus that only had a few small fibroids attached to it. Cervix—gone. The left ovary had been encased in my colon, perhaps for as long as a decade. Dr. Lowe had dissected the poor thing away from its captor and, lucky for me, had not perforated anything. The shriveled ovary with its scar-tissued fallopian tube—gone. The right ovary—healthy—I got to keep.

I feel my mouth start to fall open as my head droops toward my shoulder. I imagine a vegetative state and feel humiliated, but my body is beyond my control. I fall in and out of consciousness, each time apologizing for the drooling mess that I have become. They tell me to stop being ridiculous; I just endured major surgery. A nurse enters and instructs me how to dose myself with morphine. I am panicked I might kill myself with the morphine, which, in itself, is a thought that makes me happy because it must mean that I do not want to die! I have so much to live for now that the mystery of my pain has been revealed and removed. The nurse assures me that it is impossible to overmedicate myself, as only a small amount can be released into the IV at a time. Brian approaches to make sure that he also understands the mechanism, a gesture that fills me with love.

I did it. I made it through. And I was right to have agreed to have it done; sure enough, there had been a reason all along for the years of strange and painful menstrual issues. Now, all I had to do was lie back, rest, and let the body work its healing magic.

OH MY, DEAR READER, THAT was so much easier said than done. There I am, peacefully asleep in my morphine nap and suddenly, I am startled awake by the raucous sound of a ranting woman. Later I would discover that this was her second day of recovery, having herself undergone a hysterectomy, and they needed her room for a birth. But at the time, I was too drugged to give a damn about anybody except me. Which, in retrospect, is actually quite funny, because she was acting exactly how I was feeling. Under normal circumstances, i.e., a "normal" roommate and a clear mind, I would have been just fine. But this woman is in a mad state, her over-the-top loud voice barking into what I would soon find out is her cell phone. She lacks anything remotely resembling an ability to see beyond her own little narcissistic world—just like me. And there we are, stuck just inches apart separated by a thin curtain, able to hear every breath the other makes.

For an hour or more I cringe at the sound of the woman's loud voice. She wants her own room and by golly it sure sounds like she's going to get it. I call the nurse in, but there is nothing she can do until 9:00 PM. I have a few hours to go. I feel helpless, and silently start to cry. And I think of the women who have it far worse than me. I think of the women without medical care, the rape victims who have nowhere to go, the homeless, ill children with no mothers to bring them soup. I repeat the

Medicine Buddha mantra over and over again, visualizing this buddha's blue light shrouding all the suffering women in the world. This prayer that continues to play in my mind is the only gesture that keeps me from screaming at the top of my lungs and becoming just like my roommate.

Each time I wake up from having drifted off into a short, morphine sleep, I get the hiccups. I call a nurse in to help me figure out why I am being tortured by my sixteenth round of the hiccups since leaving the operating room just eight hours earlier. It was the gas they had pumped inside of me. The sound comes through me uncontrollably, and not without pain. My bikini line has a fresh six-inch incision, and the physical act of a hiccup is enough, I fearfully imagine, to rip those stitches wide open. The loud and angry woman lying in her own recovery bed just inches next to me doesn't complain about the noise that I am now making. I don't apologize.

Stuck in that hospital room with no hope of leaving, I lie there imagining what it must feel like to be paralyzed. I cannot even begin to contemplate how some people live like this forever. I am aware now that in that hospital room I was a person who could not picture herself ever being out of pain, ever being able to urinate on her own, or roll over in bed without help. I know now that there are far worse situations than the one I went through, but at that time, I had never been slit open, never had body parts removed, never been catheterized, never been on a morphine drip to get me through the night.

Though I had lived with chronic pain for years, I was ill prepared for the kind of acute pain that comes with a major surgery. It is obvious to me now that my surgeon, or her staff, should have detailed what to expect post-op. I could have signed up for chat rooms or read blogs. But I didn't. And the truth is, I can now admit, I actually didn't want to know.

The light comes into the room on the second morning after my surgery. The catheter is still Velcroed against my thigh. The nurse soon enters to remove it because they cannot release me until I can urinate on my own. I sit on the toilet in the bathroom that does, in fact, look like it has not been remodeled since the mid 20th century. And I sit. Nothing comes out, not a single drop. I do that mental game of willing the mind to make the bladder release, but still nothing comes out. The nurse knocks, enters, asks how I'm doing. Tells me to sit a little longer. She turns on the water because everybody knows the sound of water is supposed to help. A few more minutes and she brings me a plastic cup of warm water, instructs me to pour it over my crotch; sometimes this helps. Glory be, a little bit of warm urine drips into the measuring pan below.

By now I have met my roommate's daughter, and the three of us are cordial. They are rooting for me, as they get ready to leave the hospital. When Dr. Lowe comes in to see my pee progress, she is not thrilled; she would like me to stay one more night. During this exchange, another older woman is wheeled in, two daughters and a husband at her side.

"No way," I tell the doctor. "I need to go home."

At the time, I believed I was incapable of making it through another night in that hospital.

I recognize her judgmental expression that conveys she thinks I'm a drama queen. She agrees, nonetheless, to let me go.

It is Thursday morning when the attending nurse, one of the only nurses of half a dozen who I felt had taken my pain seriously, guides me in the wheelchair down the shining hospital hallways toward the entrance. I gingerly push myself up and out of the wheelchair, and the nurse helps me baby-step my way to our car that is waiting at the curb. "Now go and live your life!" the nurse calls out. "Be happy!"

I wave goodbye, my mother and father trailing behind thanking her for her kindness.

We caravan—my husband and me in one car, and my parents in theirs—to the pharmacy, where a shopping bag of meds waits for me. One pill to mask the pain, one to help me urinate, another for the inflammation. Oh, and one prescription formula to help me take a poop, just in case, because the nature of the surgery would not allow the body to "bear down," a nurse had told me, as one would during a "normal" bowel movement.

Inside our bedroom, I see that Brian has prepared me a throne. A small wrapped box perches on one of my many pillows. He smiles when I look at him and his eyes glisten. He has been, albeit wordlessly, terrified. I know this only now, because I can see relief spread across his whole being. This is the man I married, and, several times during those first two-and-a-half years, wished would disappear. I realize how common it is, especially for couples who marry later in life, for the first few years of marriage to play out like a ballroom dance lesson gone bad, stepping on each other's feet and unwittingly hurting their partner. But here we are, three years in and transformed by the power of commitment, perseverance, and love. We both know now, on a deep and unspoken level, that as a result of my hysterectomy, our life together will never be the same.

Inside the beautiful satin-lined box rests a rose quartz pendant in the shape of a Buddhist sword. Its silver crown boasts a small rectangular-shaped amethyst couched in silver spirals. A few tears spill from my eyes when I look at him again as he helps me climb up and onto the bed. "Thank you," I say.

"I thought you deserved a symbol of your strength," he tells me. Rose quartz is considered the stone of love and the pendant is shaped to help remind me that I have the power to cut away all future obstacles. The worst is over. "You did it," he praises. "I'm proud of you."

The house was spotless when we all arrived. And this man does not make a habit of cleaning. I realize in that moment of releasing into the comfort of my own bed how my husband's compassion has manifested: not being with me those two long hospital nights probably forced him to think about life without me. His kindness reveals that he too is shifting. The edge he had worn the weeks prior to my surgery is gone. A delicate softness drapes him in glorious compassion. I have no choice: I have to let him take care of me. Being the control-freak that I am, allowing my husband to care-take is going to be a new and challenging experience.

Getting to the bathroom from our tall bed proved a lesson in patience and strength. A patina East Indian bell that had been my grandmother's sat on the bedside table, but I could not bring myself to use it. By the second day, Brian figured out how I could get out of bed without using the bell or tempting the stitches to rip. He went into the garage and pulled out an old rock climbing rope he had saved from his premarital days of active living. He tied the rope to the doorknob across the room, and then made four knots at various spots. He draped the rope from the foot of the bed to where I could reach it. When I needed to get up, I would find the rope, and crawl from knot to knot, pulling myself up with the strength of my arms instead of my recently sliced-clear-through abdominal muscles. Not a single woman at my doctor's office had warned me about the many difficulties of recovering from an abdominal hysterectomy. All they had said was, *Take it easy. You'll be up and about within a few weeks. Don't lift anything over ten pounds for the first six weeks. You'll be driving in two, back to work in six. Don't worry, you'll be fine.*

But I wasn't fine. By the end of the week I still couldn't urinate. Not a drop. Brian gathered me up and drove me to the doctor where after an hour waiting with my feet in stirrups, they finally got a catheter that could be inserted. Ah, the relief! I lay on that doctor's bed for forty-five minutes, as urine drained from my bladder. When they insisted that I take the thing home with me for the weekend, I threw a hissy fit. I knew it was my fault for not agreeing to stay that extra night before my hospital discharge; if I had, I probably would not be in this position. I was angry, scared, and upset for Brian, who would have to deal with my bitching and moaning.

Still, I agreed to endure the catheter, and after a while actually was grateful not to have to get up. Extreme rest nourished my body while I lay in bed for the weekend, a gift that all women should give themselves on a regular basis. I discovered the deliciousness of watching the clouds come and go across the blue New Mexican sky, the delight one can know in lying blissfully still just listening to chants on an old boom box. I drank in the feeling of our typically feral cat cuddled up next to my recovering human body. My mind emptied automatically, just like my bladder when given the opportunity to release itself without having to think. That weekend was a slice of heaven I rolled in, like a horse after a long walk that sinks to the earth and dirties itself, only knowing the cool feel of letting go.

Two weeks after Brian had delivered me to the doctor's office to have the catheter removed, however, the urine was stuck again. This time it was really bad. I knew it. It was a Saturday morning, and I had spent a sleepless night with a swelling belly and an ache I knew was growing toxic. As soon as the sun came up, I called the doctor and got the recorded number for the on-call physician. When I spoke with her, she told me to get myself as quickly as possible to the E.R., as it sounded to her—not to alarm me—that I was headed for permanent kidney damage.

I walked hunched over out of the bedroom and down the hallway where Brian was just waking up in the extra bedroom. "Get up," I said. "You have to take me to the E.R."

We waited in that remodeled part of the hospital, anxious and unable to focus. My husband's patience confirmed to me what a great choice I made those four years ago when I looked into his eyes in a London restaurant over Indian curry and said, "Yes. Of course I will marry you."

As I sat in agony, waiting with great anticipation for some-body to drain my bladder, actually looking forward to having a catheter shoved into my urethra, I thought back fifteen years to the post-op appointment when my first surgeon had suggested I get pregnant to halt the endometriosis. In pain and hypoglycemic, tired and, well, just emotional, I started to cry. In that weak moment, waiting in that Emergency Room, next to a young mother who had just brought in her fevered newborn, I could not keep away images of the child that had once grown inside of me.

TWELVE YEARS EARLIER

Halfway into a ten-day yoga teacher training in February 1995, I began to feel that something wasn't quite right with my body. I was spending most of the lunch breaks napping at home just a mile away, and I was devouring a surprising amount of food. One afternoon, I realized that I had not had a period for months. Though missed periods were not too unusual considering the endometriosis and its history of causing irregular menses, for the past two years or so I had been casually dating a musician ten years my senior, whom I will call Carl, who insisted that birth control pills were poison; it was possible I was pregnant.

Part of me felt giddy thinking that in less than a year, I might actually be a mother. Though I would never have been able to admit this thought very loudly, I believe on some level that I wanted to be pregnant, thinking perhaps this would make him commit to me and I could live out the happily-ever-after little girl fantasy that floated around somewhere deep inside of my buried thoughts. The more rational side of me, though, didn't believe this scenario would ever come to fruition. First of all, Carl almost never ejaculated, having explained to me that sex for him was some kind of *tantra* practice. Secondly, we hadn't been together since December, and by now, he was sleeping with somebody else. Signing up for the yoga workshop had been a way for me to take my focus off of him and concentrate on my attempt at a spiritual awakening. Denying the possibility that I could be pregnant also provided me with a way to escape what, as the Buddha would say, was in front of my face.

Several days passed before I had summoned enough courage to drive to the drugstore and select among the many options a non-generic pregnancy test, because we all like to believe that, though more expensive, the brand-name pregnancy tests are more accurate. By now the idea of being pregnant had become kind of exciting, and maybe I really did want to see a + show in the little indicator window. With a project like taking care of an unborn child to focus on, I made myself believe everything in my life would finally be okay. But the test came up negative. I let another few days pass before peeing onto another plastic strip. This one also was negative, which left me feeling both relieved and depressed.

Then I started to replay those last few December sleepovers. I remembered that one night he had made an executive decision to send his sperm inside my womb. Despite the negative tests, it was indeed possible that I was pregnant. I made an appointment at the San Diego Women's Health Clinic for a blood test, just to make sure.

A doctor came in to speak with me after my blood had been reviewed for chorionic gonadotropin (hCG), the hormone that is produced by the placenta of a pregnant woman. She sat next to me on the bed where I was still lying naked underneath a flimsy paper robe. *Uh-oh*, I thought, *this can't be good*. If my blood had been free of hCG, the nurse who had drawn it would have returned with a smile and a "no problem." Instead, this is what I got: "Yup. Looks like you're preggers, alright."

Preggers?

"Now," she said holding my hand, "you need to decide what you want to do about it."

She then asked me when I had started my last period. I couldn't exactly remember, but I was sure that I had not had a period in months.

"We don't do abortions here, but I'm sure you can find some places in the area that do. Good luck."

She left me on my back as fear spread through me like wildfire. It was February 14 and the irony of that date filled me with such sadness. That was when it all came rushing back.

It was late one night around mid-December 1994 and I had locked the door and gone to sleep. I was living then in a large one-bedroom apartment a block from Moonlight Beach in Encinitas. Sometime in October, the relationship with Carl, whom I had been seeing on and off for nearly two years, had improved; we had stopped fighting. So when he asked for a key, I had given it to him. That December night I heard the door open. As I crawled out from under the bed covers, he took his jacket off and tossed it on the couch.

"It's midnight, what are you doing?"

"You don't mind, do you?" he asked and kissed me on the mouth.

When he walked through my door that late December night, I let him stay. We drank tea and he talked about the recording session he had just finished. He was really excited and felt compelled, for some reason he didn't explain, to share his enthusiasm with me.

By the time we headed to bed, it was late, and the sex was as mundane as it gets. Except for one thing: he came inside me, which he had never before done. He rolled over and fell asleep, while I lay in the dark staring at the ceiling. Not more than five minutes passed when I felt a warm giddiness rise up from my belly to the crown of my head. It did not occur to me to worry that I had ovulated four days previously, because in the many years since I had become sexually active, I had never gotten pregnant.

By February 14, however, his affections had turned to a new woman. It was Valentine's Day, and instead of receiving a dozen roses, I received the shock of my life. There was no way he would want to have this baby. What was I going to do? The first thing I had to do, the right thing for me to do, was to tell him. I gathered myself up and drove to his studio, where I slowly passed the café across the street. I peered in the window to see if he was having coffee as he usually did in the morning. Sure enough, he was seated in clear view. After I parked the car a block away, I walked to the café, my heart pounding out of my chest. I entered through the side door and surprised him as I sat down in an empty chair at the small table.

"What is it?" he snapped.

I couldn't speak.

"What? Why are you here?"

"I'm pregnant."

"It can't be mine."

"You're the only person I've been with," I managed to quiver out.

"Well … what? I don't know. Take care of it!"

I had nowhere to go. So I drove myself home, threw myself on the floor, and cried. And as I cursed and screamed the asshole ex-boyfriend, and myself for not being assertive enough to let him have it, I shouted all the things I wanted to say to him, but had not had the emotional strength to do so. What a loser I had been, allowing that jerk to dictate whether or not I used birth control. What a complete fool I had been letting him into my life, and into my door that one fateful night.

When I had worn myself out enough I left the pity party and realized I needed to come up with a plan. I was more than seven weeks' pregnant, and time was running out. Then I remembered the name of a woman I knew from a New Age bookstore in Carlsbad where I used to work. I had kept her phone number for some reason, and the next day I phoned her at home. She didn't know Carl or have negative feelings about my relationship with him. I knew she wouldn't give me the grief any of my family would have if I told them the predicament I was in, and that's why I turned to her.

"Stargaze," I said, "you may not remember me … "

She did remember me. Without hesitating, she assured me that we would take care of this together. She knew of a couple who had been trying to have a baby since the day they married seven years previously. They had given up, and had been looking for someone like me, older, (seemingly) more responsible, not drug addicted, etc. She told me that she would call them and arrange a meeting. In the event, however, that I should just temporarily not want to care for the baby until I could get my life a bit more in order, she offered to foster it for as long as I needed. Plus, she coaxed, I could have as much time with the child as I wanted, and promised me that their home would be open to me 24/7. Despite the temptation of the fostering offer, I decided to at least meet with the couple.

A few days later, I showed up at a local Thai restaurant feeling uneasy but excited. I was heading into what seemed like a win-win situation. The couple treated me to a nice supper, and we discussed the details of what would become a six- to seven-month relationship. They agreed to pay all doctor visits, my gym membership dues, and supply me with a $300 per month stipend. They were a very sweet couple, grateful to be sitting with me, the potential future mother of their baby. Upon leaving the restaurant, I told them that I would think about it and phone them before the end of the week.

That night I actually felt okay. I rested well in my isolation, feeling relieved to know that I would be taken care of. The next morning, though, a thought occurred to me: in order for me to be able to pull this off, I had to get the father's permission. Having an attorney as a brother, and knowing how volatile Carl could be, I would surely need a signature releasing his parental rights. But, considering he told me to "take care of it," I didn't foresee a problem with him agreeing to the solution that I had found.

When I phoned him to let him in on the doings of the last several days, his voice screamed for me to be reasonable, and wait for him to come over so we could discuss this. To me, though, I *was* being reasonable. I hung up the phone, sat on my couch cross-legged, and anticipated a fight. He stormed in trying not to show how angry he was in a stilted bad actor sort of way. He sat down next to me and explained that giving his child away was not an option. "You know how important family is to me," he said, reminding me of how hard he had tried to get custody of the little girl that his ex-wife had given birth to ten years earlier. He had suffered a grievous battle that ended poorly, no longer being allowed to visit his out-of-state daughter. He threatened me that if I went through with the pregnancy, he would just have to marry me, which was something he really did not want to do. This sounded ridiculous to me. Insane. *What an asshole*, I thought.

I wondered if he had the right to forbid me to give my child away. I did not want to ask my brother, the attorney, because he hated this guy more than anybody. I could not bring myself to talk to my parents about it either, simply because I was too ashamed.

Looking back on this devastating situation, I have incredible regrets. I had allowed that overbearing cult figure of a boyfriend to take complete control of not only my body, but my entire future. In allowing him to make the decision for me, I gave up what turned out to be my one chance in this life to give birth. I cannot imagine the woman I was then, someone so weak as to have allowed him that much power over me.

A few mornings after my supper with the infertile couple, he called and in an uncharacteristically kind tone asked if he could come over and have a chat. Hesitant, because I knew him well enough to expect some kind of manipulation, I told him fine. My heart was clamped tight, though, and as I waited for him to arrive, I told myself to stay firm. I knew what my options were, and I didn't want him to influence any decision I would make.

I opened the door and, sure enough, he was no longer angry. In fact, Carl, right there in front of me, had morphed into charming and began acting like the dream man I had always fantasized about. He told me that someday, when we both were more prepared, he would take me to a quiet island and we would create a child consciously. He would build me a hut where I could find solitude whenever I liked, and the three of us would live happily ever after, growing organic vegetables underneath the warm sky. He told me that now was not the time, and that it was important for me to do exactly as I was told. The first thing I had to do was find a doctor to give me the abortion. *Okay?*

I was a gullible, dependent, naïve girl, desperate to believe him. He pushed me into a corner; he was going to do whatever it took to keep me from giving birth and I was not strong enough to fight him. In my passive and dependent state, the only way to get through this was to believe that the future life he was conjuring was more than a fantasy. "Okay," I said and fell into his arms. He stroked my hair and kissed the top of my head.

"I'll call you later," he said before kissing me again and walking out the door.

Wow, is all I could think. *What's gotten into him?* I felt safe now. I had just been reassured that I was loved, and that indeed someday he would be the father of my child. So I got out the list of doctors that the nurse at the clinic provided and went to look up the phone numbers so I could make an appointment for an abortion.

"How many weeks are you?"

"Um, about nine?"

"I'm sorry; we don't perform abortions later than eight weeks. And by the time we get you in, you'll be at least ten, maybe even eleven. Good luck. There are not a lot of doctors out there willing to perform such late abortions."

It took me half a dozen calls to find a person who would agree to perform the procedure. $300. *Well, it serves him right,* I thought, wishing it would cost $1,000.

Saturday arrived with a rare Southern California downpour. As I took the morning to clean my apartment, the newly attentive boyfriend announced, with duffle bag in hand, that it would be a good idea to hang out with me for a while.

"Just in case."

"In case what?"

While closing all the blinds, he explained that now that I had rescinded my intention to give my child to the infertile couple, the Christian Right was going to come knocking on my door. Paranoia followed him for five days and nights as he leashed me to him like a dog. He brought me food, answered my phone, and dragged me with him to downtown meetings and studio sessions. In my love-blind vision, I wasn't even aware he was just trying to make sure I would go through with what he wanted me to do. I interpreted his affection as some kind of miracle love, even though in the back of my mind, a voice whispered that this was a convenient lie I needed to tell myself to cope with my ambivalence about the abortion.

In looking back on that week of waiting, what disturbs me the most is that I felt extremely happy, and it was only because the man I had loved for two years was finally acting committed to my every possible need. I was not aware how short lived his transformation would be. If I had been conscious of his manipulations I am fairly certain that I would not have gone through with it. And this sickens me.

Thursday morning arrived much too quickly. He couldn't hide how impatient he was feeling as he hurried me out the door to get something in my stomach before I underwent a procedure that would include my taking a sedative. He took me to a café where I choked down a poached egg and some toast. Silence accompanied us all morning as I felt him slip away. I could tell he had had enough of me by the short tone of voice he used when he urged me to eat even though I felt sick to my stomach. He started to close himself up like a butterfly returning to its cocoon. Maybe we both were feeling bad about what was about to happen. More likely, he just wanted to get it over with and move on.

I was in a haze as we drove down the 5 Freeway and headed east when we reached the 8. Following the directions I had written on scrap paper, he took us through monotone streets dotted with monotone buildings and low-income housing. The gray sky above hid all signs of decent life; the abortionist's office was not located in the best of areas that San Diego has to offer.

We took the elevator up to the third floor and entered the doctor's office like mice. We were both obviously feeling ashamed of something, I for volunteering to kill the life that was inside of me, he most likely for being the one that put me in this position.

We waited for several minutes in an empty lobby until a nurse asked me to follow her. He asked the receptionist how long this would take, and then promised me he'd be back long before we were through. Once inside a little office, the nurse took my blood pressure and other vital signs, then sat down and told me there were some questions she needed to ask me. "Are you sure you want to go ahead with the abortion?"

I sat for a few moments, shocked at the question, but did not allow myself too long to think about it. I had been pregnant for two-and-a-half months and for the last ten days had not been able to think of much else. Though I still felt reluctant, I had to let it go. "Yes," I finally said. "I'm sure."

So she gave me a Valium, told me to change out of my clothes, and left the office for a while, urging me to try and relax. About fifteen minutes later, groggy and dressed in a thin cotton gown, I slowly followed her down the hall to a cold, drab room where strange equipment sandwiched an ER-looking bed covered in white sheets. I stepped up and lay back on the bed, as a gentle voice whispered, "Hold onto my hand, this will all be over in just a few minutes." A loud machine started up. It sounded like the very first vacuum cleaner ever invented. I grabbed the nurse's hand as the male doctor entered and asked me if I was ready. I nodded and turned my head away as the sucking sound grew louder and my heart felt dead.

Suddenly, a pain worse than any I had ever experienced shot through me like I imagine a bullet would, except that this pain lasted forever. Soon I was screaming and attempting to curl up in the fetal position. I was crying as the bullet continued ricocheting off the walls of my womb like a nuclear handball game. I screamed for my "boyfriend," begged the nurse to go get him, because I just knew he could massage my back or something to help the pain diminish. I also wanted him to see what he was putting me through, wanted him to know how horrifying an abortion is, perhaps so that he would never make another woman go through one again.

I lay there breathing like a woman in labor. Within several minutes the nurse brought him into the room. I pleaded for him to do something about the pain. Gingerly he put his hands on my shoulders and pressed down more tentatively than I would have liked. He just wasn't getting it. He had really fucked things up this time. What a useless wimp, I thought, as tears rolled down my face.

After the sucking stopped, the doctor announced, "All done." Carl left my side and headed out of the room.

The nurse helped me to my feet and led me to where my clothes were waiting. I very slowly got dressed, making sure the pad they had given me was securely stuck to my underpants. A few minutes later she came back into the room and told me what to expect in the coming hours and days. She handed me a piece of paper with guidelines written on it in case I was too medicated to remember our conversation.

When I entered the lobby, Carl approached me with a sweet-smelling flower he said he drove all over the place to find; it was a tuberose, and he had not seen one since the last time he'd been on the Islands. He held my arm as we walked out of the office, and after we were settled back inside his car, he leaned over and kissed me. "You did good," he said. I didn't respond. Instead, I sat with my head against the window, and my hands over my abdomen. Even though I was in pain from the procedure, I felt like I had done the right thing. I had made him happy by following through with what he had asked me to do, and it was done. Now maybe, I told myself, we could start over and be a couple the way I had always wanted.

On the way home, he stopped off to get me a hummus sandwich and carried it in where he saw me into bed with the TV remote by my side. The pain, though not bullet-like, was still throbbing as he left the apartment and told me he would be back later. Early evening, he returned long enough to ask me how I was doing and to pack his duffle. I knew he was thinking that he had done his duty, and now wanted some time to himself. He told me he just had to have a little space, so he was going to Mexico for a few days. I didn't protest, even though leaving right then for a surf trip to Baja was as selfish and narcissistic as the pretend compassion he had shown me over the last week. Clearly, he was the only one here who had gotten exactly what he wanted.

"Bye," I whispered from the bed as I heard him leave.

Once he was gone the pain began to heighten. Perhaps the severity of the contractions was due to the fact that I had gone through with the abortion even though the pregnancy was near the end of its first trimester. Perhaps the little life hadn't wanted to leave me. Guilt I had not anticipated throttled me.

For the next few days I cried for hours at a time and bled onto pads that I threw out one after the other hoping not to find a missed piece of fetus on the cotton. After about five days, the pain subsided. But Carl was nowhere to be found. He had vanished like the baby that had once grown inside me.

BACK TO THE E.R.

Lying on the hospital bed behind a curtain, I cannot keep memories of the abortion away. I feel tears fall down my face and neck and don't have a tissue to wipe them dry. The nurses have left me alone and I feel just awful. Even though the catheter starts to drain my bladder, bringing much needed relief, I still feel disgusting. I have to lie perfectly still or a strange pinching sensation burns inside of me. A doctor will soon check me for infections of the kidney or bladder. *Why is this happening to me?* I should have gone to the doctor days ago to be checked. But because I had not been adequately educated on what to expect after surgery, I hadn't known I was in trouble.

My child would have been eleven years old by now, I lay there thinking. But now the chance for childbirth is gone. What would have happened if I had allowed that pregnancy to go full term and given the baby to that infertile couple? Would the endometriosis have disappeared for good? If so, I would not be lying here two weeks after a hysterectomy with a tube sticking out of my peesh dripping urine into a bag with measuring marks praying for the number to be high enough to go home without medical equipment strapped to my thigh.

When the doctor enters and takes a sample back to the lab, I wait some more. Urine continues to slowly drain. I feel a little better. Especially when soon the doctor returns and tells me that all I have is a bladder infection; my kidneys have not been affected. She writes a prescription for antibiotics and sends me on my way.

CHAPTER THREE

LETTING GO AND OPENING MY HAND

Nine months before my hysterectomy, nearly a full year before my husband and I would seriously pursue the idea of adoption, I had a pretty wild dream.

We have adopted a foreign baby. She is a year old and wears a white crocheted garment. On the first day that we meet, we are in an open-air market and suddenly we have become separated. When I come upon her, for some strange reason I ask, "Did somebody change your diaper?" To my surprise, she speaks. "Yes," she says. "Well then," I go on, "do you just want some cuddles?" "Yes," she replies. I scoop her up with my right arm and am tentative; I have not held a baby in so long I am afraid that I might hurt her. Then she starts to speak in Chinese, full sentences. "What does that mean?" I ask. She looks me straight in the eyes, and with the sweetest of smiles, whispers, "Open your hand."

At the time, because adopting a child was not on my mind, I was convinced that the dream was trying to tell me something else. I followed the dream's clue and decided to explore the symbol of the Chinese term "Open your hand" using the I-Ching, an intuitive tool I consult from time to time. In my search for an answer, I discovered the meaning in a question posed to Master Deshimaru, a Zen monk.

> *Every great human has said it: "I am absolute nothing."*
> *When we realize that we are exactly and no more than*
> *the result of the influence of our environment, that in all*
> *this there is no room for a me, that our life is without*
> *permanent substance, then we are open to the dimensions*
> *of the cosmos, we can receive its energy and we can create.*
> *Open your hands and you will receive everything, even*
> *material things. Don't be afraid.*[1]

I had this dream during a significant time of my womanhood. I had been so unwell for so long, I finally came to accept that I would never be healthy enough to parent a child. In the dream, perhaps the adopted baby was giving me permission to let go of what I had been hanging onto for so long: tolerating physical pain so that I could maintain the fantasy I might one day in this life, in this body know what it feels like to give birth. In this journey to health, my interest, capability, and willingness to adopt would slowly unfold.

After surgery, when the healing began, as the antibiotics ran their course and the amount of painkillers I consumed diminished, the light at the end of the tunnel I hadn't even known existed started to shine straight into my soul. I could see that rather than destroying my womanhood, removing the damaged parts from inside of my body actually opened the door to a whole new definition of what it means for me to experience life as a woman. True, I would never experience giving birth, but certainly this did not mean I could never be a mother.

I was able by now to sit in a chair for short spurts and took the opportunity to check emails and news headlines daily on the desktop computer in my office. I felt calm and was experiencing a world of possibilities. I had no agenda during the first three months of my healing, which allowed new ideas to surface. My husband and I had been fed up with the administration in Washington, D.C., for years, in part because the war in Iraq had become a daily emotional hammering. We told each other that if another Republican won the presidency in the next election, we would feel compelled to leave our country. Maybe we would move to France for a while. We had friends in Barcelona; maybe we would rent a flat there, enjoy the sea and a lifestyle more conducive to creativity and spontaneity. Or maybe we would give back to the world and serve in the Peace Corps. The world was a wide-open arena now that I was on the mend, and I wasn't just going to lie back and sleep the years away.

While surfing the web one morning, exploring the options for adventure, it was as if that little girl from my dream whispered into my ear. I watched my fingers type in a search: *International Adoption*.

"What are you doing?" Brian asked. He had walked into the office without me knowing. I tried to hide what was on the screen, but it was too late.

"Um, nothing?"

He pulled up a chair and looked over my shoulder.

"Dina ... "

"What?"

"What are you doing?"

"Well, I was just looking around, thinking maybe now that I'm getting healthy ... "

He continued to look over my shoulder as I went from one adoption website to another, from agencies to foundations to informational sites. Because my recovery was still relatively fresh, my stamina was slim. After a short while I got up to leave. "I'm going back to bed."

"Okay, honey. Can I get you anything?"

"No thank you," I said. "Enjoy!"

Brian stayed at the computer for an hour or so while I returned to bed, closed my eyes, and drifted into a deep afternoon sleep.

When I woke up, I lay still for a while enjoying the return to my body after having been out there for what felt like hours. I opened my eyes just as I heard a light *tap tap tap* on the open bedroom door. I turned my head as my husband came in and sat down next to me.

"Well," he started. Brian has a beautiful smile and just then he was grinning like he had discovered a new star in the night sky.

"What are you thinking?" I asked.

That morning we discussed how we were going to live from now on, now that I was no longer going to be ill half of every month. He had grown disillusioned with painting canvases that nobody was willing to buy. And though my practice as a writer's coach was still fulfilling, I knew I wanted more out of life. Brian and I, simultaneously, had reached a place where, now that we didn't have to focus on my health, we wanted more from life. It was like a cloud lifted and we could look beyond my day-to-day pain management. We were in love with each other more than ever. But now, without the struggle to find physical comfort, space had opened up. And with this opening we recognized that there was a void.

Over the past four years of being in a relationship together, we had spent a considerable amount of time working on ourselves as individuals, as well as working on our marriage. We had experienced some ups and downs, as many couples do in the first few years, and we worked at it. Brian pursued various means of inner work, including intense self-exploration via reading, journaling, and therapy. We also went to couples counseling, which was very helpful, as I too needed to learn how to work as a team player. And here we were: still together, and happier than ever. We had grown— together—and after taking stock of where we were with our careers, we realized that we wanted more. More than just "me me me." More than, "How can I make more money, be a famous artist, win a national book award?"

Though the pursuit of fame and fortune seems to be a real developmental stage in the Western world, filling up one's twenties and thirties with passion for and pursuit of career advancement, many people, by the time they reach forty, realize that there is something more "out there." We finally came to accept that we were middle aged and *not* rich and famous, and that it really didn't matter anymore; we had our health and we had each other.

"What are you thinking?" He hit the question back to my court.

"I don't know," I said softly. I did not want to lead him in any way.

Now, as my husband sat on the edge of the bed next to me, he explained that he could not stop thinking about a session he had had about a year earlier with a respected Santa Fe astrologer. A few days earlier, he had listened to the CD that had been recorded during the session, and heard the astrologer's encouragement for him to find a more socially interactive way of life, one that included more than painting canvases in the solitary confinement of his home studio. Though the astrologer did not think abandoning art was a good idea, and that painting would always have to play some role in my husband's life, he confirmed for Brian that he did need to find a way to be more engaged with people.

Brian had not been, and still was not, close with his own family. He had no intimate relationships other than the one he had with me. The astrologer's insistence about his need to cultivate *relationship* resonated with him. Brian realized that our life together had to change if he were to make this happen. He had to start doing things very differently.

"So," I asked him now, "what do you want to do?"

He held my hand and took a deep breath. "I think you're healthy enough to handle this now," he said. "Let's adopt."

And the journey began.

For two people in their mid-forties who have never before seriously considered being parents, to suddenly, at the same time, discover that we did not want to get to the end of our lives and not have a child to share life with, our decision to adopt felt like discovering we had become pregnant without really trying. We were excited about the possibility of such a huge life change, but cautious because we did not know where or how to begin the process.

As JOANN VESPER, LCSW, a social worker and board member of *Attach* (see www.attach.org), told me during a phone interview, "It is rare that I meet somebody that goes about international adoption in a logical way." We were no exception.

After we agreed to explore the idea of adopting a child, our search for the right adoption agency began. Before selecting an agency, however, we had to decide if we would adopt a child from the United States or go to another country. Choosing from where to adopt is one of the most important decisions parents can make. Not that one child in need of adoption is more important than another, but the journey to get that child has a thousand paths. Picking one way over another makes every adoption its own unique experience. Knowing as much as you can before you begin will help you complete your adoption without a single regret. It's been a long haul since those early days when our journey of adoption began, and I have learned so much. Most assuredly, there are things I would have done differently had I known then what I know now. (See Appendix C for how-to information about adoption.)

ONE QUESTION BRIAN AND I were frequently asked before we came home with our internationally adopted daughter was, "Why aren't you adopting domestically?"

This is a legitimate question, to which I now reply, "It's a long story. Read my book." To explain how we came to know we did not want to adopt from this country takes more time than most people have. Before we went through the process ourselves, I often wondered the same about families who went outside of the United States to adopt their child.

I think it is pretty common knowledge that the U.S. foster system most of the time takes in children who have been removed from an abusive home situation. Some people have the calling to parent these children, usually older couples who have already raised their own biological children. Not always, though. We knew that it would be cheaper to adopt a child from the foster system, but most available kids are older, and with us being in our mid-forties, the issues we would need to commit to would likely be extensive. If we wanted to use this system to become parents of a healthy toddler, we might have to wait years.

The main reason Brian and I did not use the foster care system to become parents, however, is because we did not feel capable of handling the potential developmental and emotional problems that are associated with a foster child. I have tremendous respect for those who do adopt foster children. These unique people are willing to take risks that we felt incapable of taking. I hope to eventually acquire the kind of patience needed to parent a child who may have special needs. Perhaps after we adjust to being parents the first time, and learn the skills needed to parent one adopted child, Brian and I will adopt again. Hopefully we will feel confident enough to do so from the foster care system.

During this time of exploring our options, I became interested in a cable TV show, *Adoption Stories*. I recorded the half-hour shows and sometimes watched them alone, and other times would ask Brian to join me. Though the short documentaries were filmed four years earlier, I didn't think that much had changed. One evening after dinner, Brian and I sat on the extra bed in the guest room and I cued up a program highlighting a domestic infant adoption. We both knew nothing about how this would happen for a couple and found the process interesting, but obviously stressful. The show followed one couple who had submitted a scrapbook of sorts about their lives. It was, in essence, one of many advertisement books from which the pregnant mother chose the adoptive couple. Sometimes, we learned, more than a dozen potential couples are vying for the unborn baby. But even though they had been chosen, there was still a chance that they would not become parents this time around, because the birth mother had a few days to make her decision; there was a chance she would want to keep her baby. In the end, the baby was born healthy, everybody cried, and the couple took the newborn into their arms and home.

"Wow," I said as I clicked the TV off. "That's nuts."

"No kidding."

"We're too old to have an infant anyway. I think I'd like to have a child at least close to being out of diapers, don't you agree?"

"Probably."

I also wondered about the cost of hiring a private attorney, and the concern over the birth mother's prenatal care. What if the baby was born with a defect, or a congenital heart problem or some other serious health issue?

"Plus," I shared with Brian, "I wouldn't want to worry about the baby's health in utero."

"Good point. Also, we wouldn't have a choice about the gender."

How true this was! Brian and I both grew up with three brothers, no sisters. Having no choice about whether to parent a girl or a boy was an obvious reason to reject pursuing a domestic infant adoption.

"Girl," I said.

"A girl would be awesome."

Having decided on the gender and that we wanted to parent a toddler over an infant or older child, it was obvious that the best way to become parents in a fashion that we felt best fit our needs was to adopt internationally. First, we needed to explore what country we would choose, which was not that simple. At the time, we were total naïve neophytes about the entire process of international adoption. Soon, though, we would become experts.

One vital source of information that we were not familiar with at the time comes from the Hague Adoption Convention On Protection Of Children And Co-operation In Respect Of Intercountry Adoption, commonly known in the adoption world as *The Hague Convention*.[2] The Hague Convention was put into place to protect children and their families from the potential damage caused by unregulated international adoptions. Additionally, the Convention's purpose is to prevent various crimes against children such as abduction, trafficking, or slavery. For a variety of reasons, I wish I had known about this regulatory system prior to setting out on choosing a country. But that's not the way it happened.

Pretty much the only thing we were sure about was that we did not want to adopt from an Asian country. For no particular reason, neither one of us gravitated to that part of the world. Plus, since there was a two- to three-year wait to adopt a child from China, we wanted to try for a program that would have a shorter waiting period, perhaps a country that was not as popular. Only later, long after we returned with our daughter, did I appreciate on a deep and sublime level how perfect our choice of countries ended up being for me.

Because at this stage of our little journey we didn't have a clue where to begin, we did what we knew how to do: surf the World Wide Web. One of our first considerations was the length of time it would take to complete our adoption. We had no qualms about adopting an orphan who would make us a multiracial family so this opened up all available countries from which to choose. One of the factors that helped us narrow our options was the required length of stay in the country of origin. For some adoptive parents, staying in the country where their child was born for a longer period of time is a positive. If a person has the time and money this makes sense. All adoptive parents should want to know as much about their future child's country of origin as possible, and getting a first-hand experience by living there for a few weeks or months seems like the best way to become educated. For us, however, this was not possible.

Since my husband is of Irish descent, and Ireland does not allow American citizens to adopt its children, Ireland was out. I, however, did have the opportunity to adopt a child that was born in a country from which parts of my family originated. I have Russian and Latvian heritage, so Russia seemed like an obvious first choice. One of my first cousins, in fact, adopted an infant girl from Russia who, as an almost-teen, seems well-adjusted and happy. But when we discovered that Russia requires two visits, the first lasting seven days and the second stay from ten to twenty-one days, Russia was quickly eliminated. The travel expenses alone would be much higher than other programs, not to mention the in-country fees for a total cost of, according to fall 2009 statistics, more than $40,000. Russian orphans also had, and still have, as much of the world is now aware, the reputation of not faring well as a result of having been institutionalized.

As we perused various websites, we became familiar with which countries in the world actually have active, legal adoption programs. Most of the popular international programs did not appeal to us for various reasons. Guatemala: closed at that time because they were in the process of becoming Hague accredited; Vietnam: rumored to be dealing with child trafficking issues and possibly soon to be temporarily closed; China and Russia: reasons stated above; Peru: the in-country stay is up to five weeks; Colombia: requires a six-week stay.

Then there was Haiti. *Haiti, hmm*, we thought. Just a ninety-minute flight from Miami, so not too terribly difficult to get to. Many orphans in desperate need of parents because few people are drawn to adopting from Haiti. (Of course after the 2010 earthquake, the world's interest in Haitian orphans has greatly increased.) In 2008, Haiti was eighth in number of adoptions worldwide, with a total of 330 compared to China at 2001. Haiti is considered the poorest nation in the

Western Hemisphere, with probably more than 80 percent of the adult population unemployed. The length of stay back then would have been about five days. And the cost seemed to be low to mid-range for international adoption, at about $18,000. So, we had our country. Now we needed an agency. Within a few days we came upon Worldwide Adoption Allies (WAA),[3] a licensed, non-profit international child placement agency that at the time, prior to receiving Hague accreditation, was facilitating adoptions from China, Haiti, Guatemala, and Ethiopia. The photographs of WAA's orphanage in Haiti appeared a cut above all the others we could find. We soon placed a call to the Haiti adoption representative, Carol, who worked from her home office in Minnesota. Carol was also the coordinator for the China program, as well as Ethiopia.

Carol picked up the phone on the third ring. I introduced myself and told her we were considering a Haiti adoption and wanted to know if she had the time to speak with us. It was close to dinner hour for her, but she said, "Absolutely," and spent the next forty-five minutes answering our many questions in as clear and descriptive a way as we could have hoped for.

When we brought up the issue of interracial adoption, she explained that she had two adopted Cambodian children, as well as two Ethiopian daughters. She told us that when she first brought her two girls home they were the only black people in their small community, and she did not encounter any trouble whatsoever. Her oldest Ethiopian daughter had just gotten married that past summer and there were more people in attendance than for any wedding in their town's recent history. As long as we had her on the phone, I grilled Carol about this issue. She was honest and said that of course there would be times when the topic of color and race would come up, but she said, and this has stuck with me, if you answer your child's questions simply and move on, in her experience, you would not have any problems.

"It's all in the way you approach it," Carol told us. "If you make a big deal out of it, then your child will make a big deal out of it. Sure, some kids will be nasty and say nasty things, and your child might come home from school or an outing having been teased about her skin color. But if YOU don't get upset, if you just discuss their experience without getting emotional, then your child will learn not to take the comments to heart either."

We thanked Carol for her time and hung up the phone, then spent several hours via Internet research learning and thinking about Haiti. We read that the lack of a stable government was ruining life for the Haitian people, and that the internal strife could be dangerous at times, leaving a beautiful country poverty stricken and filled with orphans.

When we saw photos and read on their website how well taken care of the orphans who live at WAA's orphanage were, we were very impressed. We made our decision. We would adopt a girl from Haiti.

Preliminary paperwork for an international adoption is a no-brainer. Usually about two hundred dollars to the adoption agency along with a short application, and you're off. The next step, however, began the complicated process that would end up taking nearly six months to complete. First we would need to find a local social worker to conduct and complete our home study.

I called a friend, an adoptive mom who owned a boutique downtown, and was able to reach her. She said she had used Catholic Services for her home study and was pleased with the way they had handled it. But when I called to get the ball rolling, the receptionist at Catholic Services informed me they were no longer conducting home studies from their Santa Fe office. We could contact their Albuquerque offices, but would have to pay for travel back and forth for the social worker, as well as for us to drive there for whatever classes we would need to complete. This didn't seem like a best option. I made a dozen phone calls to various adoption agencies in northern New Mexico and I was told by all that they had nobody to recommend, as they had been using Catholic Services. Several times we were told to contact our adoption agency for referrals.

That would not work for us, however. Our Minnesota agency with their main office located at the other end of the U.S.A. could only provide information for their own local resources. They said to try the Yellow Pages, which I had already done. I called my friend back and she put me on hold. One of her employees picked up. She had an interesting accent I could not place. Like my friend, she was an adoptive mom to a Chinese girl and had used a local private social worker named Barbara. She gave me Barbara's phone number and as soon as I hung up, I called and left a voice mail.

Later that night Barbara returned my call. She told me that the next adoption class was not going to start until after the New Year; she was too busy completing the paperwork for several home studies that were due before the holidays. Further, she was shooting for at least three couples to be in the class; only two had signed up. She also told me that we would have plenty to do before attending class, which was spelled out in the startup packet she would mail us the next day. We did not have to pay her $1,200 fee until we "graduated" from the ten hours of class. It was mid-November, and Brian and I were eager to get started.

The home study paperwork arrived in two days and was daunting. Letters of recommendation from several friends and one family member, financial statements, the dog and cat would have to have a check-up and have the vet sign off on paperwork, we would need complete physicals, and this was just the start. Our local notary, Jay, who owned the Postal Annex, would come to know us more intimately than any stranger had a right to. Luckily, at that time we lived in a close-knit community, and Jay knew my husband from his old post office days. He was so supportive of our adoption that he rarely charged us to notarize what would end up being dozens of documents.

Come the end of January, after finishing the home study sessions at Barbara's home office, our adoption honeymoon was over. The two other couples that had originally signed up had decided to cancel at the last minute. Brian and I sat through the classes solo, which turned out not to be much fun at all.

Upon entering her office the first of our four days of classes, we could not help but notice the very large ceramic elephant she had placed in the middle of the room. Everyone adopting a child of a different race is required to spend a certain number of hours discussing interracial adoption. Because Barbara knew that we had our mind set on an interracial adoption, she focused heavily on this issue.

Her lessons included a multiple-choice quiz that utilized different colored marbles illustrating the number of people of color we socialized with on a regular basis; role-playing; and watching ancient VHS videos depicting young African-American adults who had been adopted into middle-class white families decades earlier. These adopted adults came across as angry. It seemed to Brian and me that they resented being brought up in what they had perceived as a secluded white community. In the video it was clear that they blamed their parents for not having made more of an effort to incorporate African-American heritage into their family life.

At one point during the two weekends we spent with Barbara, she told us that if we indeed ended up adopting a black child we should consider moving or adopting two. Her reasoning was that it would be less difficult for our child growing up if she were able to see people who looked like her on a daily basis. Barbara believed that the child would feel less isolated if she had African-American playmates.

This news crushed me. Of course it made sense, but we were not prepared to move. And, becoming parents for the first time to one child seemed daunting enough. At that time, we were not open to a sibling group. After our last afternoon session with Barbara, Brian drove us back home in the dark. I kept silent as a stone. We were very discouraged. Once home, I felt angry toward our social worker for popping our balloon. We had gone into the idea of adopting a child from Haiti with great passion. Instead of her congratulating us for our motivation, she slapped us with that ever present elephant in the room that nobody likes to talk about: race.

"Remember what Barbara also said," Brian tried to comfort me.

"No. What?" All I could recall was, *Move or adopt two.*

"Adoption is never the best choice for anybody involved, the birth parents, the child, or the adoptive parents. But, it is better than leaving that child where she is."

Yes, I did remember those words. And I felt good about our decision. I disagreed with Barbara despite her perspective because Santa Fe actually has a fairly racially diverse population. This region includes Hispanics from all over, Native Americans, and a growing population of African-Americans, not to mention the community of adopted children from all over the world. No, I told myself, I would not let our social worker, as experienced and educated as she was, discourage us from moving forward. I refused to accept that racism would be a significant part of raising a child here. But if it ever did come up, we would handle it as responsibly as Carol has with her children.

Of course we studied the recommended books, which told us to expect racism would be an issue. Inevitably, somebody would point out the fact that our daughter is black and we are white. The books encourage white adoptive parents of black children to be prepared. Naturally, we would want to do what we could to understand how to openly deal with inappropriate comments. Further, the books raised our consciousness about various practical issues that parenting a black child would entail, such as maintaining healthy hair and skin.

For us, with an international adoption, it was also imperative that we learn as much as we could about our future daughter's birth culture. This might include artwork, cooking, and her native holidays. Because we weren't really concerned about our daughter being the victim of overt racism in our ethnically diverse community, our main focus was to establish our own family rituals that would foster and maintain our daughter's pride in her cultural heritage. Brian and I were going to concentrate on developing a bicultural family, rather than focusing on the potential problems that others have pointed out, which could arise simply because we were different colors.

One afternoon I called Carol to check in, now that the home study was finished. We were rapidly collecting the required documents for the dossier, which would be submitted to Haiti upon completion. It was likely that we would be ready to send the package within weeks.

"Well, adoptions in Haiti are taking a little longer than they were when you started this."

"How long?"

"You're looking at eighteen months from the time your dossier is in Haiti."

"What?"

"Yeah, Haiti adoptions are fairly slow. But, you're allowed to visit your child once you've accepted a referral. And you can know that while they are in the orphanage, they're getting very good care."

How I felt in that moment must be similar to what a woman feels when she calls her fertility clinic and is told that her IVF treatment failed to get her pregnant. It felt like the rug had been pulled out from under me, and there I was lying on the floor staring up at the ceiling wondering how I was going to pick myself up.

At that point, though, it really wasn't about me. Wasn't it harmful to the orphaned children to be introduced to strangers who stay a week, begin to bond with them, only to have them leave? Especially the older ones who are more cognitively developed? Maybe with an infant it would be okay, but proportionally speaking, there aren't even that many infants placed in orphanages in Haiti.

This news disappointed me to the core. Once we had made the decision to be parents and were now in the middle of gathering the piles of necessary paperwork, waiting two years seemed unbearable. It was very difficult to have had our hopes raised so high for something that was to be just around the corner, and then to be told that the corner is miles away. This experience would later make me think about the couples that have gone through multiple miscarriages and failed IVF treatments. My empathy for them heightened during my experience of this "failed" Haiti adoption.

"Wow," I said. "This is just not what I expected to hear."

"I know. I'm really sorry."

The conversation halted for a good thirty seconds. What now? Then it hit me that WAA also had an active program in Ethiopia. I wondered what the wait time was for this country.

"I am so glad you asked," Carol said. "I'm not allowed to steer you in any direction, but I think switching to the Ethiopia program is a great idea. It's a country in such dire need. And I have loved being the mom to two Ethiopian daughters. They are such a beautiful people, inside and out."

"Okay. What's the wait time for Ethiopia?"

"Adoptions are moving very quickly there, and it's possible that you could get a referral as early as three months after you submit your dossier. You could have your child home by the end of the summer."

"Really?"

"Absolutely. And Dina," Carol continued, "the need in Ethiopia is enormous. The amount of orphans there is staggering."

"What about the AIDS issue?"

Carol assured me that a full medical exam is conducted for every child brought into WAA's care, and if HIV were found, we would know about it in advance of accepting a referral. While I cannot say that this would be true for me today, and I feel slightly embarrassed to admit it, back then as first-time parents-to-be Brian and I were not mentally or emotionally prepared to adopt an HIV-positive orphan.

Since then, we have learned so much, especially about AHOPE for Children, a non-profit organization, founded in 2002, whose mission is to serve the children of Ethiopia, with its emphasis on caring for HIV+ orphans. According to its founder Kathryn Pope Olsen, in 2005 the Centers for Disease Control and the U.S. State Department decided that HIV is a manageable disease and that it was okay to start adopting HIV+ kids out of the country.

"We were one of the first orphanages to receive the anti-retroviral drugs in Ethiopia," Pope Olsen said during a phone interview with me in late 2008. "We were planning hospice when we began. We don't even think like that anymore."

In addition, AHOPE's Community Outreach Program enables orphaned children to remain within their extended families. "There has been a huge change," she said. "Our program is moving in a different direction. We are trying to assist families in Ethiopia. We have a community outreach program that assists what is left of the family…" (www. ahopeforchildren.org; see Resources).

To help encourage us to consider Ethiopia, Carol explained that there are plenty of healthy parentless children in desperate need of adoption. She said that the wait was much less than it would be if we were to continue with WAA's Haiti program. The stay in country was the same, about five days. (In spring 2010, however, the Ethiopian government made it mandatory for prospective parents to travel to Ethiopia twice.) So what if the trip itself would be more challenging? In the whole huge scheme of things, did it really matter if the transit time was nine hours or twenty-nine? This was our future daughter we were talking about, and this would be a forever choice. Carol had stated her case for an Ethiopian adoption, and I was feeling like I might just be on board.

"Let me talk to Brian about this. He's been doing a lot of reading and is already quite attached to the idea of Haiti. We will call you in a day or so."

I hung up the phone feeling confused. I had gotten myself all worked up about adopting from Haiti. I wondered if it would be difficult for me to make the switch to Ethiopia, not to mention how my husband would feel about this. As I had predicted, Brian was not happy. In fact, he was really annoyed. Brian is not the kind of person who attaches easily, not to a person or to an idea. Once he committed to adopting a child from Haiti, though, he was even prepared to study Creole so that he could better communicate with our eventual toddler. He had been reading guidebooks on Haiti and was exploring Internet sites. When our agency sent us the book by Tracy Kidder, *Mountains Beyond Mountains*, about the well-known Dr. Paul Farmer who was helping to change the lives of the people of Haiti, Brian devoured it. Naturally, after putting so much energy into the idea of going to Haiti and adopting one of its orphans, it would take some time for him to shift gears.

Within two days, however, he agreed that we did not want to wait two years to adopt a child. Before calling Carol to find out what we would have to do to switch programs from Haiti to Ethiopia, Brian went online and researched this devastatingly poor country. He read up on the rich history of Ethiopia and discovered that he was fascinated with how ancient a place this African country is.

The oldest hominid that has ever been found, named "Lucy," is a 3.5-million-year-old relic that was discovered in 1974 at Hadar in Ethiopia.[4] Lucy has been made even more famous now by an international traveling exhibit, *Lucy's Legacy: The Hidden Treasures of Ethiopia*. This five-million-year-old country is filled with stories about the Queen of Sheba, King Solomon, and the Ark of the Covenant. Brian and I were enthralled with Ethiopia's amazing history.

More influential to our decision to adopt a child from Ethiopia, however, was its amount of orphans. The numbers are too huge to comprehend, and it was ridiculous for us to think that we could make a dent by bringing home just one.

According to UNICEF, "Ethiopia counts one of the largest populations of orphans in the world: 13 per cent of children throughout the country are missing one or both parents. This represents an estimated 4.6 million children—800,000 of whom were orphaned by HIV/AIDS."[5]

Once Brian and I made the decision to sign the necessary paperwork that would officially change our program from Haiti to Ethiopia, there was no going back. By April, our dossier had been translated into Amharic—the official language in Addis Ababa, the capitol of Ethiopia—and sent off. We made an appointment with the Department of Homeland Security, U.S. Citizenship and Immigration Services (USCIS) office, in Albuquerque where we paid a large fee and were fingerprinted. Now that the United States had ratified the Hague Adoption Convention, two new forms had been introduced, and one of them, the sixteen-page I-600A, *Application for Determination of Suitability to Adopt a Child from a Convention Country*, required that we submit the form, pay the fee, and wait for approval.

Soon after we went through this protocol, we received a confusing and disappointing email from WAA, a generic announcement that we had been assigned a new representative. Her name was Aurora and she would be in touch. After becoming so attached to our adoption guide, we were informed that Carol would no longer be our representative. Since the ratification of The Hague Convention by the U.S.A., there were a slew of agency reorganizations around the country. This was very unsettling to us because Carol had been our only contact with WAA. We knew that she was our advocate, and had come to rely on her good nature and accessibility. I didn't have a very good feeling about the situation at all. Later, I would kick myself for not more definitively trusting my intuition.

When we talked to Carol about the new arrangement, she was angry as well. The news that she would no longer be in charge of WAA's Ethiopia program was just as shocking to her; she was just as upset as we were to learn she would not be finishing our adoption journey with us. The excuse given was that since she was also in charge of WAA's Haiti and China programs, there simply was too much work for her to do. The new Hague Convention regulations had created more work than was feasible for her to carry out.

Though the reasoning did seem plausible, what the bureaucrats in charge of this decision failed to understand, or at least acknowledge, is the close relationship that often develops between adoptive parents and their agency representative. We saw no reason why Carol could not have followed through with her open Ethiopian adoption cases. Yanking Carol away from us at that juncture of our journey felt analogous to what a woman must feel when she goes through her pregnancy with one obstetrician only to discover when she goes into labor that some other doctor is there to deliver the baby because hers went on vacation. How could our agency not get it? Why couldn't they have anticipated that this sudden transition would have sent us into a tailspin? We had bonded with Carol. She had become our friend. And, she was our main resource about Ethiopian children, having adopted two orphans from there herself.

Maybe this does not happen with larger agencies. Maybe this only happens from time to time, and ours was a rare case. Nonetheless, knowing that we would be completing our adoption with a stranger, well, this was quite disconcerting. Maybe we weren't as flexible or easy-going as we should have been during this part of the long process. In any case, as first-timers, we perhaps over-relied on our relationship with Carol. For the next few months, things with our new rep would at times be challenging. In our eyes, she was on probation. She would need to prove to us that she not only was as involved and helpful as Carol had been, but that she also had the skill to maneuver us through the challenging maze of what turned out to be a very tricky international adoption.

THERE ARE MANY DETAILS I have learned on our adoption journey that I wish I had known prior to starting. It seems to me that there are aspects of adopting your first child that parallel what a woman experiences going through bio-motherhood for the first time. Much of the entire process is filled with unknowns. All of us mothers-to-be have similarities, in that unpredictable events arise, occurrences for which in no way could we have planned. In addition, even if a person were to read all available blogs and publications about becoming a parent, as human beings we naturally imagine how things will be and often create expectations that may never be met.

What I know for sure now is that the journey of adoption, like some bio-mom stories I have heard, is often a bumpy road. On this path to parenthood, we all need to educate ourselves as fully as possible and learn how to be more flexible. Though the metaphorical first, second, and third trimesters are obviously different for an adoptive parent-to-be, certain phases do exist, and each one comes with its own symbolic forms of morning sickness, worry that you can't feel the baby kick, and pelvic pressure.

In the end, all of us future mommies, no matter how we are achieving motherhood, need to open our hand and not be afraid.

CHAPTER FOUR

THE PROCESS BECOMES PERSONAL

I n even the easiest, most straightforward international adoption there will be stressful moments, particularly for first-time adoptive parents. From what friends have told me, I know this also to be true for easy pregnancies—especially when a couple is awaiting their first child. There are books that help soon-to-be bio-parents by preparing them for the fairly routine experiences one goes through when pregnant. However, you can never really prepare for the unknown. From what I hear, the nine months cannot go fast enough; until she is holding that healthy baby in her arms, even the calmest, most easy-going woman will experience some anxiety.

A similar process occurs in an international adoption. No matter how smoothly the journey goes, there will be some anxious moments, which are not likely to disappear until you exit the U.S. Embassy clutching your newly adopted child's visa.

While complicated international adoptions don't generally involve life or death issues like a high-risk pregnancy, enduring the stressful wait, which is often filled with totally unforeseen obstacles, can turn your excitement about the future addition to your family into a nightmare. These difficulties can range from annoying delays to heart-breaking setbacks.

Like all governments regulating international adoptions in their country, before allowing you to adopt one of their beautiful children, the Ethiopian government will request you to have certain things in order. Due to the sad fact that children in poor countries are known often to be presented as orphans when they actually may have at least one living parent, on November 13, 2008, the Ethiopian Ministry of Women's Affairs began requiring additional documentation for adoption cases in which a living birth parent or parents has/have abandoned their child to an orphanage. The regional social affairs bureau is required to authenticate the letter issued by the local Kebele court (the smallest administrative unit of Ethiopia, similar to a ward) that acknowledges the abandonment. Oftentimes it can take weeks or months for a U.S. adoption agency employee to scour the countryside in an attempt to find a living relative. In the event that an aunt, uncle, or grand-parent is discovered, he or she would be required to sign the Ministry's paperwork. In part, this is why adoptions can take so long. A relative can show up to stop the process at the last minute if word has gotten out that one of his or her family members is going to be adopted. Further, if blood relatives *are* discovered, one of them must attend the court hearing to verbally state that the pending adoption is uncontested.

Sadly, this regulatory process is not working as well as its creators may have hoped. Where there is a penny to be made, especially in a place where poverty is so extreme, people will commit immoral and/or illegal acts if they know it will help feed their family. Because I do not walk this road of poverty, I cannot really understand the decisions some people choose to make. Therefore, I cannot judge their actions. It's a philosophical, moral, and maybe even political problem that will not easily be fixed.

Our contract also stated that before the agency would allow us to adopt a child, we were to sign a legally binding document which acknowledged that we accepted the referral and return that document with the last payment of $7,500. Once we accepted a referral, WAA's contract promised to email us updated photographs of the child every two weeks. Not only is this practice supposed to assist the future parent with the bonding process, but also these photos provide the prospective parent with the opportunity to see that the child is maintaining or even improving health in the orphanage.

Because WAA does not have an American staff member living in Ethiopia, several annual visits are made to their two care centers to supposedly ensure that things are running as smoothly as possible. At the end of May, 2008, Aurora flew there for one such visit. In addition to checking in on her staff nannies and the kids, and handling other administrative duties, her plan was to personally accept into WAA's care a few newly abandoned children. She was hoping to be able to get us our referral after this trip, but could not promise us a thing. Hope, not a promise, is as good as it gets with international adoption.

While in Ethiopia, Aurora emailed us with the news that she had admitted two girls to their Mekele foster care facility, located about five hundred miles north of Ethiopia's capital, Addis Ababa, the location of WAA's other orphan care center. One girl was perhaps age six, give or take six months or so, and her photograph was attached. Because the younger one, about six months old, did not yet have the WAA medical clearance, Aurora was not allowed to attach a photograph; she wasn't supposed to have even indicated that there might be a baby girl available. But because we were becoming first-time parents, she very much wanted us to choose the baby, for a variety of reasons, but especially because she thought I would regret never having the experience of parenting a baby. In her opinion, this child did not show any visible signs of being HIV-positive, or she would not have even mentioned her in the first place. She would have only offered us the older girl. We trusted Aurora and believed in our hearts that she really was looking out for our best interest. If we told her that we wanted to pursue adopting the baby, all that would be left to do is follow WAA's protocol and confirm the baby was healthy by having a blood sample tested.

Here is where we thought that working with a smaller adoption agency provided some benefits. Because Aurora had adopted a baby as a first-time mother and said how much she would have missed out had she not done so, she encouraged us to go that route. She knew that the older girl was at the high-end of our desired age range and that while we had not originally put in for a baby, given that she could not say when they would next have an available girl within our desired age range, she pushed us to choose the baby. Her reasoning made sense to us. I understood and respected her for sharing her opinion. But, unfortunately, she failed to remind us not to get our hopes too far up because the baby's paperwork was not yet compiled.

It is true that Brian and I had originally requested a girl aged three to five. Five was a stretch, and six would be beyond the age with which we would feel comfortable. A baby seemed very difficult at our age, considering there would be diapers and anticipated sleep issues, as well as all the other infant chores that we believed would be too difficult to master. So the choice that Aurora was asking us to make was not easy. On the one hand, if we chose the older child we would likely get to travel before the rainy season began, which was just two months away. Our adoption from start to finish would have taken less than eight months. Further, there was too much uncertainty surrounding the baby to know for sure that we would even be able to adopt her. On the other hand, we were not very excited about adopting a child of six. It seemed absurd that we would make such an important decision, probably the most important decision of our lives, and not be one hundred percent enthusiastic. Aurora gave us only a few days to make a decision, so we had a lot to think about.

After discussing the options with our social worker Barbara and a few friends and family members, we sat down and had a long talk with each other. The reasons why we had no confidence in our ability to successfully handle an older adopted child came from what we had learned in the pre-adoption classes. Here we were taught about the attachment issues that often accompany an adoption of an older child. In some cases, such as foster adoptions, or the highly exposed

2010 Russian debacle, the behavior problems are so severe that the child is returned. In addition, with international adoption, health problems in older children can be more challenging, simply because they have lived longer without proper nutrition or nurturing. Brain development may not be as advanced due to the years of malnutrition, as well as an increased chance of immune system complications.[6]

After much contemplation and reflection, we agreed that Aurora's desire for us to experience raising a toddler would be the best choice. Once we wrote her that we had decided to pursue adopting the baby, our minds and hearts rapidly caught up with our decision. Now we wanted to make it happen as quickly as possible. The rainy season would soon begin, and the courts would close for two months. It would be so unfortunate if the baby had to spend an extra eight weeks in foster care. I also worried that the older she got the harder it would be for her to leave her nannies and connect with us, yet another set of caregivers. With each passing day, as the baby's medicals did not show up, I became increasingly nervous. Without this vital piece of paperwork, WAA would not even offer us this referral.

We were excited, no doubt about it. And Aurora was thrilled that we had decided on the baby. She assured us she would have no problem placing the older girl. Shortly after this original pre-referral, however, she contacted us to say that there had been a setback; when the baby's blood was taken and the results were put in a file, before WAA had been given a copy, a staff member at the care center had stolen the paperwork.

"Excuse me?" I said.

"I know."

"What do you mean her file was stolen? Why? Who would do this? For what possible reason?"

All Aurora could say was that she was deeply sorry. Corruption happens in Ethiopia all of the time. The accused, she told me, may have done it for money, so that he could bribe her to get it back. Nonetheless, our adoption for the moment came to a halt. They would have to re-create the file now, which would include getting the baby's blood drawn again.

Journal Excerpt 6/19/2008

Dear Baby Girl,

Without a photo, without an official referral, I cannot imagine you will one day call me Mommy. I keep thinking about the woman who gave you life and how the baton is trying to get into my hands.

I think of you in your crib in Mekele not yet knowing my face. Not yet recognizing my smell or my voice as I call you when supper is ready: "Baby Girl! Time for supper!" I cannot wait to read you bedtime stories and remind you from where you came. I will always encourage your dreams to come true, and continue to pray for your country. It makes me sad to know that you have to endure another blood test. I hope and pray that it goes smoothly for you.

WHAT WE WOULD HAVE TO go through to bring our daughter home was a long road. During this pre-referral stage of our process, we wanted to learn as much as we could about Ethiopia. In addition to knowing about the birthplace of our daughter, whoever she turned out to be, we were interested in the country's history, culture, and customs. It was important to us to one day be able to speak intelligently to our daughter about her birth country, but we also wanted to be somewhat prepared for our upcoming travels there. The research we had conducted prior to choosing Ethiopia over Haiti as our adoption country was not enough. Now it was time to really dig in.

One of the most important books to read when considering an Ethiopian adoption is *There Is No Me Without You*, a journalistically slanted memoir by Melissa Fay Greene, adoptive mother of five Ethiopian children. WAA sent us a copy of this book after we switched to their Ethiopian program. The story chronicles the life of one Ethiopian woman who started an orphanage for HIV-positive children, but also includes the author's journey of adoption and her intricate work as a journalist regarding the orphan catastrophe in Ethiopia. I spent many nights reading into the wee hours only putting the book down to cry myself to sleep, sometimes with sad tears, but other times with heart-opening tears. This book opened my eyes to the profound and selfless work with which some people have filled their lives. It also helped me feel proud that my husband and I had chosen to adopt a child from a country where such humanitarian efforts were being pursued.

Another medium we used to learn about Ethiopia was films. For example, my brother told us when an episode of *Bizarre Foods* on the Travel Channel was going to profile Ethiopia. As I am a somewhat picky eater, the show made me a bit worried about what I would eat when we eventually went to get our daughter. But it also showed us what a beautiful country Ethiopia is and how friendly the people are.

At one point during the many weeks of waiting for our referral, Aurora sent an email announcement for a PBS documentary called *A Walk to Beautiful* (http://www.walktobeautiful. com/), which was filmed in Ethiopia. In this award-winning and gut-wrenching 2007 film, the viewer learns about the single most devastating consequence of "neglected childbirth": the obstetric fistula, which is estimated to occur as a result of childbirth complications 9,000 times a year in Ethiopia, where there are 59 ob-gyns and 1,000 midwives for a population of 77 million, compared to in the United States, where it does not happen at all.

It is quite common in the countryside of Ethiopia for a girl as young as twelve to be forced into an arranged marriage by her parents, who are perhaps eager to be free of the responsibility of providing for her. At that age the girl's pelvis has not fully developed. When she becomes pregnant, and does not have access to a hospital to facilitate the birth, the young mother may be in labor for days. The baby might not be turned the right way. Too often, her baby will die before it is born, but sometimes she gives birth to a healthy child. In the process, however, her little body has been deeply damaged. Not only has an internal hole formed between her vagina and her bladder or rectum, leaving her incontinent, but she also may eventually develop nerve damage in her feet and legs. Leaking urine and sometimes feces, she will be from then on ostracized by her village, and is often abandoned by her husband. With nothing to live for, the girl now simply waits for death. If the baby survives and there is nobody to help with childcare, raising the child on her own may not be possible.

I sat through *A Walk to Beautiful* in the privacy of our comfortable bedroom twice in one week, each time with a box of tissues at my side. It is hard to express the heart-ripping emotions that this film elicited in me. I felt lucky to be an American citizen, even with all of the problems that our own health care system has. I felt fortunate to have money for health insurance, and the opportunity to visit a qualified doctor even for the most minor symptom. Mostly, watching this documentary created in me an ever-more determined attitude to adopt a girl from Ethiopia. If there had once been a doubt about adopting from this country, that doubt no longer existed.

AFTER FOUR WEEKS, WHEN IN my mind it should only have taken days, I sat in my office—soon-to-be baby's room—with pen in hand at my desk. Anxiety had attacked me during the night and stole my sleep. I could not stop thinking about why our adoption agency was taking so long to offer us the referral. How long could it take to draw blood and have it analyzed? I tried but failed to come up with the reason why the process was going so slowly. Looking back at those pre-adoption days, I had no clue about, or respect for, the medical and governmental systems in Ethiopia or how long it would take to re-create that file. My attitude and behavior started to look like the stereotypical bossy American that I despise. I did not accept the concept of *When in Rome do as the Romans* and let things play out in their own time, in their own way. Again, something just didn't feel right in my gut.

My suspicious mind began to create a scenario between what we had been told by Aurora and what perhaps was really going on. I wondered why, if they had to take this baby's blood again, could there only be one hard copy in one file housing the results? Why didn't Aurora immediately get a copy of the first test for herself? At least have a phone conversation or a written statement via email sent to her from the foster home or clinic in Mekele? I felt that something was not right, and the more I thought about it, the more obsessed I became with finding out what in the hell was going on.

THERE ARE SOME READERS WHO may interpret my nature as one of an addict, and I would be the first to admit that throughout the adoption journey some of my behavior was indicative of a person obsessed. The way I see it now, I needed to stay detail oriented as a way to stay calm; that was my method for coping with the uncertainty. I kept copious notes and sometimes couldn't rest when an idea that I could not let go of popped into my head. I had blinders on and I honestly believed that there had to be answers to my questions that simply were not being offered. However, to give myself some credit, I *have* heard about and have read numerous accounts that expose corruption in the world of Ethiopian adoption. Though much of what is known today was still behind an opaque curtain, back then my radar was up.

Because Aurora was the only person I had access to who might be able to provide some answers for me, I emailed her. (At least I had the self-discipline not to call her while freaking out.)

In the letter, I asked why the blood test results hadn't gone directly to her or anyone at WAA. I knew they employed a staff nurse, so why hadn't she been able to email Aurora the results? Not having an American employed in Ethiopia certainly was causing some setbacks, and I started to think that going with a small agency was perhaps not the best choice after all. The tone of my email to Aurora was definitely pushy, and after I sent it I did feel nervous. I probably should have just saved it in the "drafts" file and counted to ten, or ten thousand, or …. But I sent it, and maybe after she read it something positive would come of it. Then again, I was pretty sure that the accusatory nature of the letter would anger Aurora and it occurred to me that she might purposely not get back to me.

Looking back, I do have to ask myself why I became so obsessed about getting WAA's so-called referral when we chose to select a child who we were told wasn't even ready to be adopted? From the very start, why didn't I take in the information that was provided as a *maybe*? Why, in my mind, had I turned only a possibility into an inevitability? The truth is that I had grown attached to a child living on the other side of the world, in a developing country, where communication to the United States is difficult at best, before I had any right to. I had let my emotions get the best of me and I would pay for it by causing myself more consternation than I could handle. Not unlike, I imagine, a woman designing her baby's room and registering for the baby shower after she has seen a "positive" in the screen of a home pregnancy test just days after a missed period, only to find that she starts to bleed three weeks later. The question to ask is this: *Why are many of us so willing to prematurely believe in something just because we want it so badly?*

But I had no time to think fruitless thoughts. It was getting late, and if I wasn't careful I would miss my physical therapy appointment. The later I arrived, the less time I would have on the body worker's table, and it was vital that I get as healthy as possible right now. I was still in pain from the hysterectomy and was having regular work done on the scar tissue. I was far from being physically ready to care for a baby, so during this phase of our adoption I needed to be as productive as possible. It was ridiculous that I was expending so much energy thinking about the baby's blood work when I myself was not totally healed.

I quickly gathered my things, grabbed a bottle of water and a banana, and headed to the garage where I was to rush into the car and drive the twenty minutes north to my appointment. But before I reached the door, I stopped by the computer one last time, and hit "send/receive." Aurora calls this *stalking your email*, but this time it worked. The blue light indicating an email is on its way gradually spread across the bar on the bottom of the computer screen. The slow-moving light foretold that something was attached and was downloading.

I saw that the email was from Aurora. My heart was pounding while waiting for the image to appear. Could the nervous energy I was feeling be compared to what a bio-mom feels when the doctor is performing the first sonogram on her pregnant belly? If so, and if she had experienced trouble conceiving in the past, her anxiety surely would be overwhelming. Is the baby healthy? Deformed? Does it have all its crucial body parts? I too wanted to see an image.

Born: November 2007 in Mekele Ethiopia
Aster became a McQueen on June 24, 2008
She weighs 18 lbs, is 56 Cm and HC is 41 Cm

Your daughter was brought into the care of WAA in May
of 2008 after her family was no longer able to care for her.
She is a beautiful, happy, and healthy little girl.

It had been exactly twelve minutes since I had sent Aurora the note that expressed my frustration. And here it was: an *official* referral notice from our adoption agency, and three photographs of our baby girl. *Congratulations Mom and Dad!!!!!*, read the email subject line.

Oh my, she sure seemed like a happy baby. She looked well cared for, healthy, and calm. Now I could relax a little because she appeared to be in a good place, in good hands. I rapidly reviewed the information, which consisted of just a single paragraph about her "social history." The attached medical report was dishearteningly illegible. However, since Aurora sent this information, I had to assume that she had received the necessary data that allowed WAA to give us this referral.

In that moment, it didn't matter that there was practically no information. The only thing that seemed to matter was her face, with its plump cheeks and toothless grin. She was nestled in the arms of a beautiful young woman and exuded happiness. *Thank God, I thought*. Our future daughter was obviously one of the very few who found her way into a small foster home, rather than being crammed into a facility where one hundred or more children vie for attention. I was back to feeling grateful that we went with a smaller agency because it looked as if in the arms of her nanny, in this small foster home, she was doing just fine. There are definitely pros and cons of both small and large adoption agencies. If and when I am asked for my opinion about which sized agency to choose, my answer will be lengthy and inconclusive.

Aurora had emailed the referral while on vacation at the New Jersey shore and phoned to verbally congratulate us shortly after. It was a Tuesday, and she told us she would not be returning to her office until that Friday. She assured us that since it was not a holiday in Ethiopia she would not be going away for the fourth of July. She promised to send us any information if there was any news to forward. Before hanging up she mentioned she would call her office to try to get them to email us a more legible copy of the medicals.

By late that night, no new medical report arrived. Because I did not want to bother her while she was on holiday, I spent a week anxiously hoping that things were still on track. Though we were excited about the possibility of adopting Aster, we couldn't let ourselves get too attached. Though our adoption was starting to feel more real, there had been too many signs that raised my doubts. Even though a new copy of the medicals was promised to arrive soon, the contract stated that we were supposed to have some kind of legal paperwork too. I had to assume that something more official should have been included to send back. Something just didn't feel right!

During the days that followed, we tried not to get too giddy even though Brian frequently kissed Aster's photograph, which was stuck to the refrigerator. "Hello cute baby," he cooed, making my heart patter. We attempted not to worry along with my mother that the baby's room wasn't ready. Though it was still possible that we would be traveling to Ethiopia by the end of the summer, at this late date it didn't seem very likely that we would be able to get there before the rainy season began and the courts closed.

At three in the morning, on Independence Day, I was wide awake. I was worried about the way things had transpired thus far and had been doing a lousy job of modulating the highs and the lows of the process. Since I knew she would be working later that day, I wrote Aurora an email.

> *… We still know next to nothing about Aster. Though we are very excited about our referral, we remain concerned because we have not been told if she has any birth relatives that could come claim her. We still do not have a legible medical report. We understand that the courts will likely be closed in three weeks, so are trying to accept that we won't be getting a court date this summer. We do not know if or when the baby's file will be complete, and so cannot even contemplate a travel date. Without any further information we do not feel comfortable sending WAA the remaining $7,500.*

Aurora emailed back, promising that she would do everything in her power to get us legible medicals, including a hard copy mailed out from the main WAA office that was located in another state. Even though she was seemingly having a tough time getting us enough accurate information so we could count on our adoption being a sure thing, this email did include new information from Africa that she forwarded. One of her Ethiopia staff in Mekele had sent Aurora Aster's birth mother's first and last names. "[Her mother] is living in Eastern zone of Tigray. Aster is 7 months old, she is very lovely."

So we had a bit more information. Knowing Aster's mother's name certainly felt meaningful and significant. But the all-important document did not show up. Until we received a medical report that we could read, with an official stamp at the top of the page, we had no business counting on this baby being our daughter. We still had not received any correspondence regarding her file getting re-created from the file that had been stolen to know that everything was still moving forward. My frustration was growing, and if I did not get some answers soon, it would turn into anger.

I decided it was time to give Aurora a call. Although Brian is generally okay not being very assertive and begged me not to "bother" her, in keeping with my character, I ignored him. I insisted that we had already paid them a lot of money, they were asking for a lot more, and we had a right to some communication.

Aurora called shortly after I had left her a voice message. She was finally ready to explain some things and began by saying that she had been in contact with the man who had been fired for stealing our future daughter's file. She had pleaded with him, via email, to give her the information. He was a father himself, she said, and she tried to appeal to his sense of fatherly love, sharing with him that we had no other children.

Aurora continued to fill in some of the blanks: Her right-hand person in Ethiopia, Tefere, was to train their new employee the next day. He had been instructed that our case was the only work he was to focus on. He would need to scour the countryside attempting to find enough information to re-create what the ex-employee had originally discovered. I recalled the conversation a week or so before when Aurora had phoned us to disclose the bad news about the file being stolen. She had told us then that Tefere was going to be the one to re-create the file, and it was going to be done pronto. Now on the phone, these many days later, I wondered what the hell happened to that plan! But I kept quiet.

It was impossible to keep thoughts of raising Aster as my daughter out of my mind. Even though I told myself not to get attached to a photograph, a "maybe," it was impossible not to. After so many months of preparing to adopt a girl, now a particular girl, from Ethiopia, it felt as if Aster represented my only chance to become a mother. The process had been too challenging to consider going through it again. During this time, Brian and I made a decision: if we could not adopt Aster, we wouldn't become parents at all. We could not imagine connecting to another potential child knowing all the while that *that* adoption might not happen either.

Okay, so here is a bit of retrospective insight about the process of international adoption: it is my belief that the manner in which adoption agencies organize the referral/ acceptance process engenders a false sense of attachment to a child that may or may not end up becoming legally yours.

And this, I now understand, creates an unrealistic sense of entitlement in the prospective parent. Our agency, in a manner typical of international adoption, sent a photograph of an adorable baby, with a letter designed to appear like a birth announcement, stating that she already had been given our name, which actually may be a marketing tool. There were far too many court documents and legal issues that had to be collected, submitted, and approved before the baby would truly be ours, not to mention the remaining $7,500 we had yet to pay the agency.

However, there is also this: though it may seem like a ploy to rein in potential parents by their heartstrings via a photograph, I also now realize the significance of an adoptive parent being given an opportunity to become attached to the "idea" of a child. Birth parents have the nine months to connect and plan and feel close to their future child. In adoption, attachment is a necessary but precarious key that unlocks the opportunity for bonding. In most cases, except Russia, wherein a prospective parent is not even offered a photo to go with the referral, a photograph of the child is all a person has.

Adoption agencies that are concerned about their clients' ability to bond with a future child should make it transparently clear from the outset that more times than not, international adoptions come with intermittent obstacles, and that the experience is almost never as quick or straightforward as anyone might predict. In other words, let the photographs and videos flow, but agencies must be sensitive to what many of their clients are bringing to the adoption process after what may be years of failed pregnancies, unsuccessful fertility treatment, or just a sense of urgency to bring home an adopted sibling for their existing child(ren). The present practices, while encouraging bonding with an orphan, run the risk of causing the prospective parents undue emotional suffering during what can be a very laborious process.

NINE DAYS LATER, WE STILL had no medicals and I had begun to feel indescribably helpless. In addition to helpless, I also was now angry. I knew in my head that we were not the only clients that had hired WAA to facilitate an international adoption, and Aurora was undoubtedly very busy as a new mother herself. My heart didn't give a hoot about those facts; I just wanted to be reassured that everything was going to be okay, that Aster would be our daughter. But Aurora alone could not promise me that, so there was really nothing more that could be done on my end except to try to learn how to accept the way things were, which, for me, seemed like an insurmountable task.

I realized also, during the time of waiting, that there was so much more WAA could have done to prepare us to expect the unexpected. They could have compiled more information about the poverty level and lack of infrastructure in Ethiopia. They could have sent along with their "Welcome Pack" testimonials from other parents who had experienced not only the good of international adoption, but the bad and the ugly as well. Why not get it all out in the open from the start? Yes, here I was, too far in to turn back now, with only my faith to get me through: faith in an agency I remorsefully realized I hadn't taken the time to get to know.

I wish I had maintained a metaphysical orientation to help me put things into perspective during the often agonizing adoption process. Such a frame of mind would have created a sense of calm and kept away at least some of the obsessive behavior. It was the absence of faith in the process, the lack of belief that what was meant to happen would eventually happen, that caused so much distress. Of course, even for someone like me who has studied Buddhism, routinely meditates, and practices yoga on a regular basis, it is not easy to sit back passively waiting for a stranger to come along and tell you it's time to travel across the globe to pick up your child.

Retelling this now, many months after we have returned home from Ethiopia with our daughter, I am able to look at matters in a somewhat different light. Because the child who ended up becoming our daughter was purported to have been born around the same time that I went through the surgery that removed my ability to give birth, perhaps this particular soul was, all along, supposed to be with us. From here on I will acknowledge that I can choose what to believe, and it is, in my mind, quite plausible that she had been waiting for me for twelve years, ever since I had made the regretful decision to have an abortion.

During our journey, however, I did not have the clarity of hindsight. I behaved exactly like myself, with the intensity of my desire to adopt this particular baby fueling my less than laid-back attitude. The situation was made more difficult, though, than it needed to be, due to what I now believe was a lack of education from our agency about the often routine delays in the process, as well as the agency not providing us with all the information we needed or doing what I had been told by our social worker was supposed to happen.

During a face-to-face meeting with Barbara, she had told us that usually there was some kind of a referral acceptance form that we were to sign and send back with the requested final payment. After looking at the limited information that WAA sent to us, she raised the horrible idea that maybe this adoption was not legitimate. This time delay, she affirmed, would not normally happen with a larger agency, one that had an American staff person living in the country where the adoption takes place.

Barbara recommended that we not send the money. She was concerned because the photograph of Aster that was attached to the original email notice Aurora had sent, which our agency called our referral, had been shot back in May with a camera that had since been stolen along with Aster's paperwork. Barbara agreed with us that there really was no proof of what was currently happening in the foster home. She said that we could no longer be certain to whom the employees still working there were committed.

Barbara further wanted to know what exactly Aurora's responsibilities consisted of. Who else was responsible for coordinating the adoption in Ethiopia? It is not uncommon, she said, with smaller agencies to employ workers that end up stealing money. "Sometimes, in fact," she told us, "there isn't enough money to feed the children."

WE DROVE HOME FROM BARBARA'S that afternoon in silence. Brian went to the fridge, opened a beer, and poured it into two glasses. We took the drinks outside and sat down under the setting sun, my husband's usually optimistic outlook visibly waning. Outside in the quiet warmth of a summer evening in Santa Fe, we shared our feelings of doubt and decided that we would do whatever we could to make sure that we could adopt Aster.

Summer monsoons in Santa Fe often arrive without warning. The summer of 2008 saw downpours that filled rain barrels to overflowing with every sudden storm. Thunder crashes announcing lightning strikes usually force me to quit whatever work I am doing on the computer and run to shut all the windows that don't open onto a portál. Surge protectors have been known not to work around here with such close strikes. One afternoon, I pushed the storm out of my mind, told myself *it won't happen to me*. But a bolt of lightning struck outside my office window, perhaps at the very moment I decided to turn off the computer. Too late. I could not get back online. No emails would be able to come or go until the computer was fixed.

After my somewhat less than considerate emails, Aurora had said that she would prefer for our social worker to be the go-between. She told me that she was concerned for me and that she wanted to make sure I was getting enough support. I took it personally and like a child decided, "Fine, whatever," and did not contact her again. But after the computer went on the fritz, I reluctantly called her, hoping just to leave a message on her voice mail to tell her that my computer was down. I wanted her to know that I would not be able to retrieve her weekly email update that was to arrive the next day. To my surprise she picked up the phone. I was further surprised to hear delight in her tone. "It's good to hear your voice," she said, insisting that she never wanted to cease communicating with me. She reiterated that her intention had been to make sure that my needs were being best served.

I told Aurora that my computer would be down for a while. If she emailed I would not get it. Her friendly voice was actually a relief. She was not angry and had never been. I apologized if I had come off as accusatory. I also took the opportunity to explain that the tone of my letters and phone messages had sounded desperate because that was how I had felt. Further, I had come to realize that what disturbed me more than anything, what was causing me such despair, was learning that a person supposedly working for the betterment of the children of his own country would actually sabotage those efforts. Even though I had traveled extensively, this had been a rude awakening. That was the part that was hurting me the most; I could not accept the destructive acts that some people commit.

Then Aurora shared something with me that sure would have been nice to know from the beginning of our rocky relationship. She took a deep breath and I sensed that she was struggling with her words. Maybe she was afraid of saying too much? Was she unsure of her role and what would be appropriate to say at this point?

"Dina," she said, "You do not have to apologize. If I were you, I cannot say if I would trust me. I cannot say that I would trust my agency. If I were you, I would probably go to bed with a pack of Lexapro," which, she shared, she pretty much had done during her own lengthy and difficult China adoption that had been completed several years before. I understood now that Aurora empathized with our situation.

"I'm not the same person I was going into this," she told me. "It has changed me." She explained that she originally took the job because she did not want anyone else to go through the kind of anxiety she endured while waiting for her little girl. She was willing to give up much of her personal life to make sure the children are taken care of. She knew it would not be easy, but she felt she had no choice; it was her mission to help get those children out of Ethiopia with as little trouble as possible. In the process, however, she went on, she had awakened to what she called the "evil" that exists in the world.

What a waste it was to have doubted this person. Had she only shared with me from the start more of who she was I would have had a different view of her. Aurora had taken on the Ethiopia program with the commitment that the children of Africa were the only ones that mattered, and that she would do whatever she could within her power to get them into a safe environment with a loving forever family. She knows first-hand how it feels to believe in human beings' inherent good and to trust, only to be betrayed by a person who cares only about his personal survival. The man who stole Aster's file was in big trouble. She promised that she would eventually call the police and he would be "forever ruined." (Which, by the way, did not give me any pleasure in knowing.) But until our adoption went through, she could not even offer him a bribe to get the file back. Because, she feared, he would continue to withhold and ask for more. If she did turn him in to the authorities, and she had seen this happen before, he could call the Embassy at the eleventh hour—anonymously—and tell them that our adoption was not legitimate. They would be obligated to stop the process until they could verify that his accusations were a lie. Aurora dealt with this kind of situation a while back when she was forced to fly to Ethiopia to facilitate the retrieval of documents for parents who, instead of staying the four to five days usually required, ended up in Addis Ababa for a month.

"You think you feel devastated now, Dina, it's nothing compared to if you had to spend three or four weeks in Addis Ababa." Corruption, poverty—it is all related. One begets the next in a never-ending cycle that has infiltrated the efforts and diminished the positive nature of international adoption.

Aurora reluctantly didn't have any new news about Aster for us. She assured me again that they were doing everything in their power to make our adoption go through. She asked me to please be patient and to call if I needed her support. She reiterated that she was there for me and to hang on.

FRIDAY AFTERNOON ON MY WAY back home from town, I stopped at the mailbox. Inside our locked box was a Priority Mail envelope. I quickly got back in the car, heart pounding, and raced the mile or so home where I ran into the house and shouted, "Mail from WAA!"

Brian met me at the dining table where I opened the envelope. Inside, finally, was the legible medical report. *HIV-negative*. There it was. Proof that WAA had a valid medical report. Proof also that confirmed we were adopting a healthy baby.

In addition, there was a piece of paper that we had not seen before, the *Child Referral Acceptance Form*, on the agency letterhead. This was the missing link that Barbara told us should have arrived with the photograph and announcement. Soon, this whole thing would be over. Since my computer was still at the "medics," I called Aurora to let her know that we received the mail from WAA. Sure enough, Aster was medically well, just as she had told us. Though much was now clarified, we wanted Aurora to tell her boss that we still were not satisfied; why were they only giving us four days to send the money along with the signed document when, according to the original contract, we should have been given two full weeks?

There was a moment of silence on the other end of the phone. "Oops," Aurora quietly said. "That's my fault."

She was supposed to have sent this *Child Referral Acceptance Form* on the very same day she sent the illegible medicals and our referral. Had that form accompanied the other paperwork, we probably could have avoided the last weeks of distress. The *Child Referral Acceptance Form* explained it all, as did the contents within. On this form there were blanks for us to fill in our names, our address, the name of the child we were accepting into our family, and the birth date we were to assign for her, given that a known date was not available.

As previously mentioned, Aurora was on holiday when she sent us our referral, and said that she did so because she knew we had been so anxiously waiting. She had bent the rules in an attempt to do something nice for us, but in sending us the documents via her cell phone, her kindness had backfired.

"I've been told not to do this kind of thing," she confessed like a teenaager being caught for forgetting to take the trashcan to the curb on garbage day. Her boss apparently had scolded her before for working when she was on holiday, because events like this can so easily occur.

"Well," I said to her, "this explains everything."

So WE RECEIVED OUR REFERRAL, finally. (A sigh of relief.) Now, it was time to get down to the business of working on a Lifebook.

During our pre-adoption classes with Barbara, we were instructed that as soon as our referral was solidified, we were to begin creating our future child's Lifebook. A Lifebook is supposed to include information about an adopted or foster child's life prior to being placed. We had been told about the importance of creating as much detail as possible, as it is said to help the child when she becomes old enough to want to know such things as why she was given up for adoption. By the time I realized that we would not be receiving any more social history for Aster than her birth mother's name and what was attached in the original emailed referral, I had grown deeply concerned about how to do this; we had nothing to put in it. I had actually been looking forward to compiling the book, not only because I had always enjoyed scrapbooking and collaging, but also because the reason for this particular art project seemed like the most important creative endeavor I would ever complete.

In much of the adoption literature I had read, which included books written by adult adoptees, it was my under-standing that as an adult an adopted person is likely to have an easier time accepting her situation if she has enough information, such as where she was born and why she was given up for adoption. I wanted to be the perfect adoptive mother to our daughter; I wanted to be the one to help her come to terms with the curiosity and possible helplessness that many adopted children eventually experience. At this point, she would know nothing. Even though much later on I would indeed acquire more information, at that time I was concerned that she might one day blame me for not making more of an effort.

We decided to have a short session with Barbara so that she could instruct us how best to put Aster's Lifebook together.

"Well, you know," she started, "because you are adopting from Ethiopia, and the information you have now is all you are going to get, you're going to have to get creative."

"What do you mean?" I asked, incredulous. She's the one who had emphasized how damaged our child might be later in her life if she didn't know anything about her past!

Without apology, Barbara simply said that we should do the best we can and not worry ourselves silly about something over which we have no control.

The next day I followed Barbara's advice and got busy. What I ended up doing is gluing into Aster's Lifebook congratulatory emails that friends and family had sent when first hearing of Aster being our future daughter. I also included the photographs that WAA had sent thus far. Over the next five months of our wait, I added photos as they trickled in from the Mekele care center. In addition, prior to leaving for Africa, I did a web search for what was going on in Mekele specifically, and Ethiopia in general, around the supposed time of Aster's birth. I figured that this would be better than nothing, and we would add items and clippings as our adoption journey progressed.

Because many true orphans are purported to be found on doorsteps or street corners, some in boxes without even a note, I started to get the feeling that a Lifebook may not be intended for children adopted from developing countries. However, I do agree that some kind of scrapbook documenting an adopted child's life before arriving into her new family may be important to facilitate a discussion about her adoption when the time comes. It was ridiculous for me to have believed that I would be able to complete a Lifebook as it was defined in our pre-adoption classes due to the simple fact that so many Ethiopian orphans lack a documented social history. It would have been more helpful during these classes for our social worker to have instructed us to document the conditions that existed in our daughter's birth country that allowed us to adopt her in the first place. It is a disservice to parents adopting from a developing country to tell them to put together a Lifebook when no social history exists.

It is my hope that social workers who take on adoption cases from poverty-stricken countries not suggest the adoptive parent use Lifebooks and instead encourage parents to create a scrapbook of sorts with a broader definition than the one that currently seems to exist. The kind of pre-adoption support that would benefit the adoptive parents-in-training would include how to communicate honest, loving support for the *lack* of information about the child's birth family. More often than not, one or both parents have died. It seems to me now it would better serve all involved to anticipate *no* information and instead counsel adoptive parents to commit to helping the adopted child know her birth culture and accept who she is as a result.

SUNDAY, JULY 27, 2008, WAS my forty-sixth birthday, and a good day it was. My husband and I spent the morning in relaxed bliss. I made apple pancakes, and the weather was perfect. Clouds floated across the sky, keeping the usual summer heat at bay, which meant we could take the dog for an easy two-mile hike on a trail we'd recently discovered not far from our house. We rested leisurely when we returned, had a glass of champagne, and headed into town to peruse a bookstore we liked before enjoying an early supper at our favorite Santa Fe bistro, the restaurant where he took me for our first date.

When we returned from supper that night, I wrote a check for $7,500, which left just enough of the previously borrowed $25,000 for us to travel to Ethiopia and acquire the necessary documents to complete the adoption. Brian and I filled in and signed the *Child Referral Acceptance Form*, and the next morning I took the package to the post office. By now, the courts in Ethiopia had closed for the rainy season, not to open again until mid-September or so. We knew we would not be leaving for Ethiopia until some time in November. Now came the work of learning how to become good parents to our Ethiopian daughter.

CHAPTER FIVE

AFRICA CALLS

O ne morning near the end of October, the phone rang. "Y'all made it. You passed court."

Though it was three months later than we originally thought we would be arranging our trip to Ethiopia, Aurora's call was a welcome surprise. There had been a good chance that we were not going to receive this news for many weeks. We got lucky. Three other families expecting to travel with us ended up not leaving for months, due to that unwritten international adoption rule: expect the unexpected. In our case, the unexpected turned out for the best. We would be able to travel before the holidays, before my parents returned to San Diego, where they spend the winter. In the end, their help was crucial, and we felt fortunate to have them here. That first week would have been incredibly difficult to manage without them.

EVEN THOUGH MY HUSBAND AND I have traveled throughout Europe, we never went anyplace where we were concerned about what we ate or how to get safe drinking water. Planning the trip to Ethiopia was causing us a modicum of anxiety, but because we knew that we would do whatever it took to bring Aster home, we didn't let our fears take the wheel.

There were two main assurances that helped us relax. The first was that we would be staying at the Hilton Addis Ababa. We looked forward to their heated pool, where we could hang out with the baby and other families. We were comforted that there were a variety of restaurant choices and 24-hour room service. It was nice to know that they had an in-house gift shop stocked with over-the-counter medicine and toiletries if we needed anything. We were also relieved that we would not run into language barriers because of the Hilton's multilingual staff.

The second major calming factor during our pre-travel weeks was that we pretty much knew exactly what we would be doing each of the five days in Addis Ababa. After we switched to the Ethiopia program, our agency sent a basic itinerary as part of their welcome packet. So, far in advance of leaving we were given an idea of what the trip would entail.

- Sunday: Arrive in Addis Ababa
- Monday: Our daughter will be brought to us and we will go to the American Embassy to finalize the adoption
- Tuesday: Optional field trip to the museum
- Wednesday: Optional field trip to the outdoor market, with a dinner celebration at a traditional Ethiopian restaurant

- Thursday: Petting zoo during the day, and a trip to the indoor mall prior to flying back to the States

Over the course of several months prior to leaving for Ethiopia and in an effort to prepare future parents for the entire adoption experience, our agency conducted several conference calls, to which we were required to listen. A woman who had already made the trip to bring her children home led some of these mandatory sessions, while Aurora conducted others. There was some important information conveyed, but for us not every three-hour training call was helpful. Each person's situation is different, and each child comes with her or his own unique issues, so advice given to a group is not always equally relevant to each listener.

For example, one call focused strictly on techniques for hair and skin care of African children. During that session, an African-American mother of an Ethiopian girl led the tele-class. Her instructions were a bit worrisome for a white adoptive mother of a black child who wanted to make sure not to screw up anything. This mother emphasized how difficult it can be for people who aren't accustomed to working with this kind of hair. She said it would take a lot of practice and patience for those of us without experience in this area. After sitting through that class, weeks prior to leaving for Ethiopia, whenever I ran into an African-American woman around town I politely stopped her and told her that we were adopting a baby girl from Ethiopia.

"I'm sorry to bother you," I said, "would you mind telling me where you get your hair done?" One local yoga instructor I stood in line behind at the Co-Op gave me the card of the salon in Albuquerque where she goes, because she said this was the nearest place to go to get African-American hair styled. Brian and I thought it might be fun once Aster was with us to regularly take the train from Santa Fe to Albuquerque and make a day out of having her hair done. I could learn by watching the experts, I comforted myself.

I would find out later, however, that people's hair in Ethiopia varies from the north, where Aster was born, to those who are from places more south. We would come to discover that Aster's hair is not the kind of hair that the woman leading the call described to us, as it is soft and curly. We wouldn't necessarily need a trained professional to show us how to do her hair.

Another conference call we were required to attend had to do with attachment and bonding. The information we studied during our months of waiting was reiterated from the first-person point of view by a mother of two adopted girls, one of them from Ethiopia. Not yet having met Aster, we grew nervous about the challenges we might soon be facing. The behavioral difficulties that this woman was having with her younger African child, I would later conclude, probably had more to do with the fact that she put her adopted baby girl in daycare shortly after returning from Ethiopia than with the one-year-old whom she adopted. But I would not realize this until after we met Aster and discovered what her particular needs were.

Perhaps the most vital pre-adoption lesson we received over the phone was the one that focused on travel itself. This call was aimed only at the parents who were getting ready to travel; the waiting parents who had not yet passed court were not allowed to listen in. We were very excited to hear all the details and made sure to take good notes. We were given the contact information for a travel agent our agency encouraged us to use to book flights, one that specializes in international adoption. Though there were some restrictions we would not have had if we booked the flight on our own, like which airlines we could use and what days we would be able to travel, the cost of the trip was far more affordable. This particular travel agent, in business for many years, is considered an international adoption travel agent and contracts with only a few airlines. Because of this, she is able to offer big discounts. In addition, as a specialized travel agent, she strongly urged us to buy travel insurance because so often baggage is lost. I would not have done this if I directly booked our flights. Also, she made it clear that we could contact her in case of travel emergencies.

Later during this call Aurora's tone turned serious. I had been communicating with her long enough to know what this voice meant: something wasn't quite right. Sure enough, she started by saying that some changes were taking place with Ethiopian adoptions. The general atmosphere in Addis Ababa was shifting, and we would not be staying at the Hilton, where we had been told from the start all WAA families stay.

Believing we would be at the Hilton while in Addis Ababa had helped me stay as relaxed as I could have been under the circumstances. The Hilton is a full-service hotel, and if we did not want to leave the grounds for any reason other than to attend the Embassy appointment, we would not feel deprived. Now, however, I began to feel some concerns that the trip could pose a variety of previously unforeseen hardships.

Sometime during the summer of 2008, Aurora explained, the Ethiopian government began requesting that adoption agencies no longer set up their families at the Hilton, where—in addition to the Sheraton—most of the agencies booked their families. She said that recently many foreigners, mostly Americans and mostly Caucasians, behaved loudly and demandingly toward the hotel staff and around the city. This, in turn, called quite a bit of undesirable attention to the fact that many children were leaving the country with less-than-respectful outsiders. Adoption is still not an entirely accepted concept in Ethiopia. She said that the local people were starting to express anger at seeing so many foreigners take away their children. Further, if the sentiment grew too much more negative, it would jeopardize all future adoptions.

Aurora spent much of the time during her last visit to Ethiopia scouting out a guesthouse where WAA families, until further notice by the Ethiopian government, would stay. She also told us that the field trips were cancelled and we would pretty much need to be sequestered in this guesthouse and not walking around the streets with our baby.

Before this call, my travel concerns were minimal. Aurora, though, assured us that we would have three meals a day prepared by a staff cook, food she promised we would feel safe eating. She also said that we would have access to a driver who would take us to the market for whatever we might need, from diapers to water, formula, or anything else. Ethiopia may be a developing country, she said, but Addis Ababa was the capital. We were not to worry about being unable to buy necessities. I had no choice but to trust her.

The detailed nuts and bolts of traveling to Ethiopia were not discussed over the phone. We learned from early website research that hepatitis A and B vaccines were standard for Africa travel, and several doses were needed spread out over the course of months, so we got our first shots right after our referral came through. But for advice about getting vaccines other than hepatitis, Aurora told us to consult our family doctor, a parent who had already traveled, and/or the CDC website. The CDC provides up-to-the-minute travel and health advisories, which supersede any advice your agency, physician, or guidebook might provide.

Unfortunately WAA failed to address—neither via conference call nor in any of their literature—the possible medical issues that may arise for many children who have lived in an orphanage. Most parents adopting internationally are doing so for the first time. After a child has been given a clean bill of health and you joyously accept the referral, you may not even imagine that she could be handed to you in less than tip-top condition. There are, however, certain common health issues that arise in children who have been living in group homes. Earaches, diaper rash, and molluscum contagiosum—a viral infection of the skin, which is commonly spread through skin-to-skin contact—are all typical conditions that kids contract when living side-by-side.

We were not told about the importance of locating and consulting a pediatrician who is familiar with common medical issues that orphanage babies and young children can pass around. This kind of specialized doctor explains what to look for in your child and prescribes antibiotics and creams to help alleviate any physical suffering they might be experiencing.

While we were unprepared to deal with the medical problems that Aster had, we at least took precautions for our own health. Our family physician gave us a prescription for an antibiotic, which he recommended that we take at the first sign of serious stomach upset. We packed analgesics, antacids, and antidiarrheals in our carry-on bags, along with a travel first-aid kit, and a portable device to purify tap water. We also brought a tube of grapefruit seed extract that can be dropped into water prophylactically to help stave off unwanted bacteria. By the time we booked our flights, I felt prepared.

IN THE DAYS BEFORE LEAVING, I had time enough on my hands to think about the yearlong process it took to make our international adoption happen. During those months we attended several gatherings, usually a barbecue, of an adoption group, all of us parents who used the same social worker. Some of the couples had adopted or were waiting to adopt domestically through foster care or from a then-popular program that facilitated infant adoptions in El Paso. Others took the international route and chose Ethiopia. Some had already brought their children home. Others, including Brian and me, were in the wait.

It was during one of these afternoon barbecues that I stood back to listen to the conversations taking place. Excitement permeated the atmosphere, from the couples who had just submitted their home study or dossier to those who had recently returned with their children. There was photo swapping and many stories shared, as well as so-called war stories. Some couples admitted that they went to adoption as a last resort. Others were not that forthcoming. We seemed to be the only couple who never tried fertility treatment to have a baby. During these get-togethers, I got the feeling that more than one of the parents, or potential parents, with whom we were socializing were not as happy as they tried to appear. At times I detected an air of sadness in the room. I interpreted this, albeit perhaps falsely, as the residual aftermath of years of failure to maintain a pregnancy and give birth. With all the heartache, effort, and expense that goes into trying to give birth but failing, it is natural and understandable that a person may see adoption as the second best way to become a parent. In the end, no one could be expected to feel elated about adopting if what they really wanted was to parent a child that came from their genes.

One night, after an afternoon spent among our adoption group, fatigue corralled my defenses, and I started to feel concerned about my skills as a mother. I admitted in my own mind, with a lump in my throat, that I had allowed myself to fantasize about the love that I would share with my daughter, that as soon as I took her into my arms and she felt my unconditional love, she would melt into me. "Mommy," she would coo, as I fed her a bottle and tucked her into bed. But at the gathering that day, I sensed what I would call a *disconnect* between some of the adopted kids and their parents, and I realized that I might be setting myself up for disappointment.

There are plenty of birth parents who aren't close to their children, so what made me think my daughter would ever love me? We knew the odds were in our favor, though, because Aster was living in a foster home with just a handful of other children. We had chosen a small adoption agency in part because we wanted a child who was provided with enough attention to avoid, we hoped, common orphan attachment problems. We were sent photos of her strapped to the back of her nannies, which made us believe that she was experiencing secure bonding. But we did not know, nor would we ever, how the early months of her life may have affected her.

Many children in foster care or orphanages become emotionally damaged by a lack of early bonding and/or attachment with a consistent, loving adult. If Aster were one of these babies, we would have our work cut out for us. This of course did not mean that I did not want to go through with our adoption. I just had to prepare myself for the possibility that the reality might not match my expectations.

As we were preparing for our trip to Ethiopia, Brian and I decided to have a four-day layover in Paris together. For years we had discussed going to Paris, that "someday" sort of song that many couples rehearse but never perform. Fanciful pictures filled our minds: oh, the cafés, the museums, the lazy lovemaking in a room at my favorite turn-of-the-century hotel on the Left Bank.

When we arrived in Paris at Thanksgiving, we were just days away from becoming parents. A constant feeling of excitement, anticipation, and even agitation accompanied our every move. With this hovering awareness that Aster was so incredibly close to becoming our daughter, we, in all honesty, were not fully present.

During those anticipatory days on holiday in late November, we continued to tell each other, "One day, we'll come back with Aster." Though it was easy to say "yes" to this trip to France, since from there it was a mere seven-hour flight to Ethiopia and we didn't know when we would get back again, it was *because* we were on the brink of meeting Aster that Paris fell flat. We had fantasized about this "second honeymoon" with such detail that we failed to acknowledge how much space Aster had begun to take up in our hearts. Already, even before having met her, we missed being with our daughter.

One night, sitting across from each other at a tiny café table, we sipped a glass of wine and waited for our small meals to arrive, *salad Niçoise* for me and a *croque-monsieur* for Brian. I remember that moment so distinctly. Jazz pumped through the speakers, and the buzz of French that I didn't understand blocked out the milieu of people around us. I took my husband's hand from across the small table and held on tightly. My eyes filled with tears.

"You know," I said, "it's possible she's not going to like us."

"Sure it is," he said.

"I'm so scared," I admitted.

"Me too."

"What if we can't do this?"

"We can. And we will. There's no turning back now."

His voice was a comfort. Of course he was right. We were going to be great parents.

"I wouldn't want it any other way," I assured him.

As we ate in silence I tried not to worry about the possibilities, the many "what ifs" I did not want to face. I realized that though we may have been well trained to parent an adopted child, there were still legitimate issues that worried me. What if our daughter couldn't get over feeling abandoned by the nannies with whom she had bonded over the last six months? What if she did not recognize us as the people called "Mommy" and "Daddy" from the photo album we sent to her foster home? What if she was not physically well enough to make the long plane ride home? And then there was our lack of training in simple parenting skills. Goodness, would Brian know what to do with a poopy diaper if I wasn't in the room? What if I couldn't remember how to change a diaper? What about bathing her, and how were we supposed to prepare a properly sterilized bottle? In all our anxiety over, and work toward, completing an international adoption, we hadn't even thought about reading some run-of-the-mill parenting books or taking a parenting class.

After our dinner plates were removed, we ordered a coffee and a slice of *tarte tatin*, a delicious kind of apple tart. "Well," I said. "I guess it doesn't matter how scared we are."

"Nope, it sure doesn't."

"This has been really special. I don't want to lose this," I said. "You know there's going to be times when I'm going to miss just me and you. The time here has been so sweet."

He smiled at me and took a sip of wine. "Let's promise that we'll always make time for each other," he said. "I've seen so many couples fail at this. Let's make a pact not to let that happen to us."

I felt a tear fall down my cheek. I couldn't believe we had come so far together. Being in Paris with him at this exact time of our lives, though maybe not ideal under the circumstances, still was absolutely perfect.

THREE HOURS PRIOR TO DEPARTURE, we found ourselves waiting in a drab Ethiopian Air lounge at Charles de Gaulle. I used our last euros to purchase a large bag of whole-grain biscuits and a plastic bottle of blended Scotch whiskey, just in case we wanted a late-night drink and snack during the five nights we'd be in Ethiopia. Finally, at 10:45 PM, Brian and I boarded the flight to Addis Ababa.

As we got on the plane, we looked at each other with expressions that intimated *Maybe we should have skipped Paris*. If we had taken Lufthansa, the airline that our travel agent had suggested, we would have changed planes in London. The Lufthansa itinerary from Paris to Addis didn't work with the schedule. The only way to make our Paris trip possible was to be exactly where we were now: trying to squeeze into our seats on an old jet with ashtrays in the armrests that were soldered shut. But Paris was a memory I am glad we made happen, a trip I will always remember with a smile in my heart. While it's obvious now that we would have been more comfortable on a different airline, our choice to spend a few days in Paris was the right choice.

We did not sleep more than half an hour of the seven-plus hours to Ethiopia; we were too excited and too nervous. Despite all the books we read, the classes we took, the phone calls, no matter how much one prepares for this moment, there is still so much uncertainty. Being older than most of my friends who became parents years earlier, I wondered, not for the first time, mind you, if we were too set in our ways. How much would having a baby affect our marriage? How much would we be at the mercy of our child's schedule? Would we have the flexibility and the patience to turn our lives over to a toddler? Though the road we had embarked on after my hysterectomy was coming to an end, a totally unknown world awaited us.

As I sat next to my husband and ordered a glass of wine with the vegetarian meal, I attempted to watch a movie. This was an opportunity to relax and enjoy myself. But my mind wandered out the window, across the sky, and into a country where I had no idea what to expect once we landed.

One of the most important guidelines we had been given by many sources was to use hand sanitizer and antibacterial wipes often while in Ethiopia. We were to use bottled water to brush our teeth, keep our eyes closed when showering, and never sit on a toilet seat. We were instructed to bring toilet paper with us on all outings and not to order drinks with ice or anything made with water that was not boiled. Even though I have traveled a lot, I never visited an area where such medical concerns were stressed. With all of these recommended precautions, I was admittedly a little frightened about being in Ethiopia.

Looking back I realize that I was more distracted than I would have liked to have been. My mind was preoccupied with irrational thoughts of contracting a disease that would make the trip even harder. I heard that one does not want to have to go to the hospital in Addis Ababa. Africa was a brand new experience for me, and I was freaking out a little.

I knew if I could only sleep, or enjoy the movie, we would be landing in a blink. But the minutes ticked on so slowly. I just couldn't wait to meet my daughter.

Once we landed and gathered our carry-on luggage, we disembarked into the stark area where we went through a short line and had our passports stamped. The agent pointed "that way" and we followed his direction assuming we would retrieve our bags before going through Customs. But through a glass door, the way he had pointed, there were no clear instructions on what to do next. It was 6:30 AM now, as we stood there dumbfounded. Naturally, we felt tired and disoriented. I looked at Brian with what must have been a wrinkled, confused brow. There was nobody around to tell us where to go to get our luggage or how to take it through Customs. Then some random guy approached us and asked in broken English if we needed help.

"Do you know where we get our luggage?" I asked.

He scurried us to a conveyer belt where we were the only ones awaiting bags. Of all the other people on the flight, it seemed odd that nobody else was waiting. My mind started to become quite busy. Not so much panic yet, but a sense of being in some strange movie. We waited as the conveyer belt started to inch its way around, and we watched the luggage slowly coming our way. How weird, I thought, our bags were the only ones coming down. Without prompting, the guy who had taken us this far grabbed our luggage and tossed it onto a cart that just happened to be nearby. Puzzled, Brian and I looked at each other, and followed the man out of that area through glass doors that opened into the main area of the airport.

"What, no Customs?" I said.

"Guess not. It would have been nice for WAA to tell us what to do when we got off the plane."

A thin, goateed man holding a sign that read "McQueens" greeted us.

"You must be Tefere," I said.

"Yes, how was your flight?"

Brian asked Tefere if we should tip the man who helped us get our luggage.

"No, from here on out, I take care of all of that."

A sigh of relief left my body, as we followed Tefere to the car that was waiting for us in the outdoor airport parking lot. As in many other airports around the world, dozens of men, young and old, stood around with eager expressions, obviously hoping to help a traveler to his car and, in return, be given a *birr* or two. Fatigue overran my body and my mind, but not enough to keep away the sadness in my heart from seeing the level of poverty here. This is the country where our daughter was born. Someday we would return to show her the land on which her ancestors stood. It was obvious, though, from the first few miles outside of the airport that this place was in dire economic straits. Clearly Ethiopia is in great need of recovery on many levels.

As I looked out the window on our drive to the guest-house, I felt glad that we had chosen to adopt from here. But even though adopting Aster was a wonderful way for us to grow our family, I began to feel a broader sense of responsibility. I knew that others who came here left with this feeling as well. Helping a country in such need is not just about grabbing orphaned or abandoned children and getting them out. What Ethiopia, as well as other depressed developing countries, needs is a worldwide recognition that the country itself requires incredible social, economic, and medical aid so that so many children do not have to leave.

My memories of this trip to Addis Ababa are not consistent with the naïve images of Africa that once occupied my mind. The reality of the conditions I saw was heartbreaking. Crowded streets with no traffic control. Old cars not required to maintain any kind of standard for emissions leave the city hazy and rank. But the people of Addis Ababa have far more to worry about than pollution control. Ecological commitment is a luxury that this kind of poverty does not allow.

I sat in the taxi embracing the sights, sounds, and smells on the way to the guesthouse and what I saw cannot be described as *poverty*. A new word would have to be invented to illustrate the true essence of this place. Though my instinct was to turn away, I would not let myself. A voice inside was shouting at me: "Adopting Aster has forever linked you to Ethiopia. Do not close your eyes." For a somewhat sheltered American girl, this was an assault.

As a child growing up I never had a desire to visit any country in Africa. But after being in Ethiopia, I strongly believe that all of us should once in our lives see up close and personal the kind of poverty that makes you cry. I was naïve thinking that it would never touch me. I was wrong. And I am, I like to think, a better person as a result.

As I sat there holding back the tears that wanted to escape, I knew in my heart that we were here for a reason. And it would be worth whatever the next five days had in store. In that taxi, with all the mess swimming around my mind, I could not wait to hold my daughter and bring her home.

CHAPTER SIX

MEETING ASTER

Before we left for Africa, WAA sent us the week's schedule, which included arriving in Addis Ababa on Sunday and meeting our child on Monday. We were so exhausted when we got to the guesthouse, it did not occur to us to ask Tefere if we could alter the plan and meet Aster later that same day.

When we walked into the guesthouse, there was a couple from Portland eating breakfast with their twin baby boys. It was a total thrill to see them all together. We introduced ourselves, and they explained that because they arrived the day before, Tefere brought their children to them earlier than scheduled. This news was motivating;

When Bitsy looked back on Jin-Ho's arrival, it didn't seem like a first meeting. It seemed that Jin-Ho had been traveling toward them all along and Bitsy's barrenness had been part of the plan, foreordained so that they could have their true daughter. Oh, it's you! Welcome home! Bitsy had thought when she first saw that robust little face, and she had held out her arms.

–Anne Tyler, from Digging to America

there was more flexibility than our agency originally conveyed. Overhearing our conversation, Tefere suggested that Brian and I rest before we made any decisions about meeting Aster. Without a moment's hesitation, we told him that after we napped for a few hours, we absolutely wanted our baby brought over from the care center. We wouldn't be able to sleep that night knowing that she was just a short distance from where we were staying.

INSIDE OUR LARGE GUEST ROOM, Brian and I floated in that dreamy space that descends after a four-hour siesta in the middle of the day. The sheer, white curtains tossed about in the breeze that entered through the open window. We lounged on one of the two full-size beds, my head resting on his shoulder. His arm felt comforting around me in our last moments together sans baby. We felt groggy, but anxious. The sound of our breath was all that could be heard inside, though outside, Addis Ababa was a bustling mix of car traffic, people walking along the dirt road, and some activity in the courtyard below. We jumped as the loud, old-fashioned ring of the telephone on the side table sounded.

"Yes, hello?" I said.

It was Selam, the young woman who ran the front desk of the guesthouse during the day, calling up to say that our baby was on her way. We bolted up and out the door.

The old Toyota sedan pulled up outside the gate and idled, with a sound like *kutchity kuchity, clk clk clk clk*, the kind of noise an uncared-for vehicle makes when it is in dire need of a tune-up. The guesthouse guard stood at the curb waiting to assist. He was young, smartly dressed in cap and button-down coat, and he couldn't stop smiling. When he opened the door of the taxi, I wanted to rush to his side and elbow him out of the way. Restraining myself from reaching in for our baby was a challenge. It felt unnatural to just stand there, but there was a certain implied etiquette required in this situation. So Brian and I stood firm, our hands locked tightly together, eagerly awaiting our first peek at the baby.

We were told that after spending the first six months with her birth mother, our future daughter had been placed in the care center in Mekele with at least two nannies and fewer than nine kids. Aurora told us several times that this baby bonded with one of the nannies more than a child usually does. When we first learned about their relationship, Brian and I felt happy for her. She had a safe and loving connection with a mother figure, which is much more than most orphaned children get. A few weeks before we left for Africa, we learned that the baby would soon be moved from her Mekele home and flown ninety minutes south to WAA's care center in Addis Ababa, where we hoped she wouldn't have to stay long before we got there. My heart ached knowing that she not only had been taken from her birth mother, but eight months into feeling connected to another woman or two, baby Aster was again ripped away from that security. I hoped so much that she would someday learn to trust me.

I saw our daughter exit the car from the backseat in the arms of a woman who I presumed was one of the Addis nannies. Aster was burrowed like a snail in its shell. She wore a bright red jumper dress that stood out against the gray of the courtyard cement. Underneath she had on a long white shirt with the sleeves rolled up at her tiny wrists. I remember telling myself to imprint this moment because I knew it would pass too quickly, and I wanted to remember. If the details weren't captured in my mind, though, it was okay; the mother of the twins we met that morning held our video camera and was documenting the event.

I saw the baby sleeping as the nanny took her first step toward us. I still can hear the sound of her flip-flops *slap-slap-slapping* and can see the depth of her smile that spread across her face and through her moist eyes. I wanted to go to them instead of waiting for them to come to us, but taking our daughter out of the woman's arms would have been rude. Maybe the nanny could see my eagerness because she moved toward us with a calm focus and a tender expression. I felt a lump develop in my chest but swallowed it because I didn't want tears to mar my first encounter with this delicate child we would forevermore call *daughter*.

The baby was still asleep as the nanny approached us. A plastic bag loosely tied and hanging around her wrist swished as she walked, its contents the sum total of Aster's possessions. The woman reached her arms out to me and I carefully, with heart beating wildly, took the sleeping child and cradled her close. She was a feather. Couldn't be more than fifteen pounds, I thought, even though according to a recent health report we received she should have weighed at least eighteen.

I looked down at Aster and saw that her hair was bundled with colorful rubber bands, perhaps a dozen or more. She was beyond precious to me, such a tiny little thing, so cute and snuggled into herself. In my arms she felt as I had imagined my baby would feel. I breathed in her smell and let tears fall from my eyes. Aster was a manifested dream I hadn't known I could dream.

I felt a bit selfish that I got to hold the baby first. This was supposed to be *our* moment, and I wanted so much for Brian to have the experience too. He was Aster's new daddy as much as I was her new mommy. So I stood as close to him as I could, hoping that maybe he would feel a bit of what I was feeling. A few seconds later the nanny handed him the plastic bag and kissed the baby's neck. I could see she was trying not to cry.

We quickly thanked her, in English, although she didn't seem to speak it. And then we tried to hug her and tell her that Aster would always be loved, and how much we appreciated all she did, even if it was only for a week or so. I am pretty sure she didn't understand, but our body language probably spoke for us. It seemed to me that she was in a hurry to get going. I was so consumed in holding my daughter that it didn't occur to me to flag someone over to help us translate some questions. As far as I knew she was the only person able to share with us what the baby liked to eat, if she had any physical needs we should know about, or what her sleeping habits were. After she said her last goodbyes to the baby, she nodded, smiled, turned and walked back to the idling car. The door slammed shut and the driver took the nanny away.

Aster's head felt luscious against my chest. Even in this bliss, though, I felt nervous. I suppose this was normal. Maybe what I was feeling in that moment is similar to what it's like when a first time bio-mom is handed her newborn and the neonatal nurse is called off to other duties. Suddenly there was a tiny person totally dependent on me and all I had to go on were my not-very-confident instincts. There was no time for me to worry, though.

Aster woke up briefly, and turned her eyes up toward mine. She blinked. Then she put her head back against my shoulder. Brian came close and we hugged, with the baby cradled between us. He kissed me. I quietly cried, and his eyes also filled with tears. In the silence of this union, I felt physical sensations and emotions I had never previously known. Even with all the spiritual practices I went through, all the seemingly intense love relationships I engaged in, I never in my entire life realized that such transcendent feelings were possible. In that moment I felt what could only be described as pure joy.

We both were pleasantly surprised that Aster was in such a deep sleep. Her calmness allowed Brian and me the opportunity to fully enjoy these first moments with our daughter. Recalling how other parents described their initial meeting with their adoptive children, either the children cried with grief over having left their nannies or were cut off from their emotions altogether, I expected the worst from this transition. We were quite relieved that it went so smoothly for us.

Soon, however, Aster would be awake. What would we do then? This was the easy part, I thought. Would she begin to cry? Wonder who the hell we were? Another new environment, with new smells, and more new people trying to keep her happy. I felt anxious but did not let my fear consume me. The minutes and hours would tick rapidly by and life would take care of itself.

With the baby cuddled safely in my arms, the three of us walked inside to the lobby, where a coffee ceremony was taking place. In Ethiopia, a coffee ceremony is a common, recognizable, and, sometimes, daily event. We read about the Ethiopian coffee ceremony during our pre-travel research and looked forward to partaking in one. The process of roasting green coffee beans over hot coals, grinding the beans by hand, then boiling the beans in a special pot twice before serving it sounded too extravagant for a host to prepare on a daily basis. But Ethiopians are a social people, with gatherings of friends a frequent occurrence. It just so happened that this week's guesthouse performance, so to speak, took place just moments after Aster was handed to us. It felt as if the ceremony was being given in honor of our new family. In actuality, it was just a coincidence.

Smoke from the roasting coffee beans billowed all around, and as the wind shifted now and again it stung my eyes. Brian and I sat shoulder-to-shoulder on one of the two tan leather couches. The couple from Oregon, who would be spending the week with us at the guesthouse, sat on the couches with their boys and kept us company. They too were enjoying the elaborate coffee experience.

As I sat taking in the moment, part of me split off and drifted outside of my skin. I saw two white couples caring for their brand-new babies, Ethiopian children leaving to be raised in America. Sitting there holding my darling daughter I felt awkward. I guess I was self-conscious for being born in America and having money enough to fly all the way across the world just to bring one child home. Though I felt engaged in the moment, the mild discomfort distracted me somewhat. Maybe I was just feeling strange holding a child that would within hours legally be mine. I felt flooded with a mix of emotions from joy to fear, awe to surrender.

In traditional dress, one of the guesthouse employees passed a tray with demitasse cups filled with strong coffee. She offered a bowl of sugar, and because my arms were full, when I nodded my head yes, she spooned some in for me and stirred. Another part of the coffee ceremony included popcorn. When the popcorn finished popping on the portable stove, a bowl was passed. Everybody took turns reaching in for handfuls and eating the small, crunchy pieces. Though I was hungry enough to devour the entire bowl, Brian had to feed me one piece at a time because I didn't want to disturb Aster.

"Someday the three of us will be doing this at home in front of *It's a Wonderful Life*," I quietly said to Brian. "Can't you just picture it?"

"Absolutely," he said and dropped a piece into my mouth.

I sat there somewhat numb. The experience could be likened to a dream because the truth of being handed seemingly out of nowhere a tiny child that was now and forever my daughter did not feel of this waking world. I was sitting on a sofa in Ethiopia with my husband at my side, my calm baby in my arms. I could not get over the fact that she rested so peacefully. With her asleep against my chest, she shrouded me in calm as well.

After I finished my second cup of strong coffee, though, I started to return to the reality that lay before us. Soon, the lobby would be clear of guests, and it would be time for Brian and me to act like the new parents that we were. Until now it didn't register that Aster was breathing with a slight wheeze.

I realized that her nose had some gunk edging the nostrils. How did I not notice this before now? No wonder she was so tired. My child was sick. I had not thought much of it as we all relaxed on the couch, but when, after an hour or so we went up the two flights of marble stairs to our room, I started to worry. If whatever she had was bad, what would we do? In four days we were to spend forty hours in transit back to Santa Fe. For now, though, there were more pressing concerns, like perhaps we should think about changing her diaper?

EARLY THAT NIGHT AFTER FIGURING out how to use the baby sling we brought with us, we went downstairs for supper where the large dining table was set for two. The other families went out for dinner, but we did not want to take our sick baby to a restaurant. Also, we were looking forward to the cook that Aurora assured us would be available.

Brian loosened the sling so Aster could rest easily on my lap. We sat down in front of the place settings and waited for somebody to show up to take our order. We were told that pasta would always be available, so we decided that's what we would eat. Easy to digest, no worries. The door to the hallway that led up to the guest rooms opened, and a thin man and woman came to the table and sat down at empty seats. They introduced themselves; they were a couple from Canada, professional runners training in Ethiopia because of the altitude. The man came every year, and had been doing so since first discovering this training method. They had been together several years, and seemed happy and committed. She shared with us that she would not be running so much on this trip because they were soon going to try to have a baby.

One of the guesthouse attendants came out of the swinging door of the kitchen carrying a large bowl of spaghetti smothered in tomato sauce and a basket of bread, which he set down in front of the Canadian couple. He picked up the plates that were in front of Brian and me, and put them back down where the Canadians sat. He looked at us with a curious expression, and then went back into the kitchen and returned with a large salad.

"Excuse me," I said to him, "What is your name?"

"Selassie."

"Selassie," I said, "I'm Dina, and this is my husband, Brian, and daughter, Aster. We'd like to have what they're having please."

"I so sorry, miss," he replied. "No possible." Selassie turned away and headed out of the dining room, through the swinging door, and back into the kitchen.

I am not being dramatic when I write that a rush of panic and confusion sped through me. I didn't know what we were going to do. I felt very angry and also embarrassed. We were so hungry. I looked down at Aster, who had a slim smile across her face as she peered up through the neck of the sling. It would not matter much to her, as we would be feeding her mainly baby formula and teething biscuits. It was getting dark outside, and Brian and I needed to eat.

I jumped up and crossed over to the front desk, my hands supporting Aster's bottom that drooped in the sling. I asked the young man working the night shift how we could get some food. He told me that there were plenty of restaurants nearby. I explained that we were told that there would be a cook to prepare meals for us all week.

"Only breakfast is included in your stay here."

"Can we hire Selassie to cook for us also?"

"I don't know. But you are free to use the kitchen."

"Wow. You're kidding."

When I got back to the table, I shared with Brian what I had discovered. I looked at the Canadians and said, "We're sorry, we were told by our adoption agency that dinner was available and we assumed this was for us as well."

"Please, sit down and eat, there is so much here, we can't possibly finish it."

"Are you sure?"

"Yes, of course. Sit. Please," said the woman.

"Thank you," I said. "That's very kind."

"Thank you," Brian said to the couple, and we sat back down.

During the meal, the Canadians shared with us that they would be leaving in two days. I asked if they knew whether or not Selassie would be available to cook for us. They had no idea, because they booked the room and board through their travel agent back in Canada.

When Selassie came back to the table, I asked him if we could hire him next.

"They do not hire me here. I find out if possible. Okay?"

"Okay, thank you."

"Maybe we should try to contact our travel agent," I said.

"Please let it go, Dina," said Brian. "We'll figure something out."

"There's a decent restaurant across the street," the man told us. "We've eaten a meal there and were able to get some pretty good pasta."

"That's good to know, thank you," I said.

"See, it's all going to work out."

I tore off some tiny pieces of bread and handed one to Aster. But she was sucking on a teething biscuit and ignored me. I alternated from taking bites of food to wiping the drool from the baby's mouth. Her focus on eating the biscuit was so cute, but the mess was extreme. I was a new mom and realized I would need to let go of my need for tidiness in a hurry.

Before leaving the dining room, Brian asked the couple, "May we help pay?"

"Not at all. Our pleasure," the man replied.

We thanked our hosts again and told them we were heading up early; it had been a very long day. As for Selassie, though he didn't end up cooking for us, over the next few days he did go out of his way to assist us. And because I was in no position to turn down help from anybody, even though I felt uncomfortable at times, I appreciated his efforts. He sanitized Aster's bottles, accompanied me to a local bank to change money, and whenever we ran into him in the lobby he asked if there was anything he could do for us. I simply assumed he was just being kind, as all of the local people we met were so nice. Later, however, we would see a different side of him.

Once we got up to the room and unloaded Aster to the floor, where she was happy to crawl about exploring the contents of our suitcases, I became angry. Had we been told that we would have to fend for ourselves for lunch and dinner all week, I certainly could have used more luggage space to pack food. I would have included freeze-dried meals, the kind one eats when camping. More crackers, nut butters, dried fruit. The more I thought about how Aurora had misled us, knowingly or not, the more annoyed I grew. I realized I was pacing and complaining out loud when there was nothing I could do now.

I called down to the front desk and asked the man who answered to please call Tefere for me and have him call me back. About ten minutes later, the phone rang. I explained the situation to Tefere, who acted astonished that Aurora told us that lunch and dinner would be served at the guesthouse. He said he felt badly that this happened and asked us if we wanted him to come over and take us out to a restaurant. I told him that we already ate but that we would certainly appreciate it if he could help us out over the course of the coming week. I also wanted to know how we could hire Selassie to cook for us after the Canadians left. Tefere told me that WAA had nothing to do with Selassie, so he had no idea. But he assured me that he would arrange to get us to a supermarket the next day to buy some food so that we could use the kitchen. I told him Aurora said not to go out in the streets with our baby, that a new regulation was instituted instructing adoptive parents to stay off the streets of Addis Ababa. He told me that was ridiculous. Not true at all. I made it very clear how disappointed we were with WAA and Aurora for being so uninformed, and told him that I would lodge our complaints with her when we got back to the States. I thanked Tefere for his attention and hung up somewhat relieved. Though Aster was oblivious to our concerns over meals, she was now getting fussy.

"What's up, Aster?" I knelt down to where she was crawling around on the floor and whimpering. "Are you hungry?" Brian was seated on the bed and came over to sit with Aster. "I think I need to make her a bottle."

He picked her up and bounced her, which was a good distraction. Then I fixed a bottle using the powdered Nestlé's formula left by the nanny, because we were told to keep her on the same formula until we could gradually introduce something new to her system. In making the formula, we were advised to use tap water, and then slowly increase the amount of bottled water. Ironically, when foreigners drink local tap water it gives us diarrhea, but locals who are used to the tap water might get sick from drinking bottled water. Prematurely changing the baby's formula and water that she was used to drinking might make her sick. We decided to follow the first suggestion, but not the second. Even if there was a chance she could get diarrhea from putting her on bottled water, it was better to deal now with messy diapers in the privacy and space of our room than in a few days in a tiny bathroom on the plane.

Though snot was coming out of her nose, I was delighted to see Aster's happy temperament. I handed her one of the two new pacifiers we had brought with us and focused on her as she sucked away. She looked up at me and offered a smile. If this tiny, ill child, I told myself, a baby who has been through more than I could ever possibly try to imagine, can look a stranger right in the eyes, amidst feeling unwell, and likely confused, and can remain at peace enough to smile, well then I can certainly handle whatever would come my way over the next few days.

THAT FIRST EVENING WITH ASTER, she spent most of the time either in my arms or in the sling. Since we didn't know how many hours she had slept before she came to us, we weren't sure how long it would be before she was tired again. Plus, she was sick and if her symptoms got worse, she might have trouble breathing. That night, even though Brian and I were exhausted, we mentally prepared ourselves for the possibility that Aster might be awake for a while. We did, though, want to be ready in case she was tired. By 9:00 PM when the crib had still not been brought up to our room, I called down to check. Soon after, two young men knocked on the door and carried the pieces into our room. They assembled it without a hitch. That was the easy part.

One of the questions I had asked Aurora prior to leaving for Ethiopia was about Aster's sleeping arrangement while in Mekele. Because we were told that from the start of her stay at the care center she slept with her nanny, Brian and I were concerned that she might not even want to be in the crib. So we planned on trying to co-sleep with Aster. I would start us off in Addis, and we would continue with the three of us in our big bed back in Santa Fe. That was the plan. Still, I felt good knowing that the crib was ready in case our best-laid plans went awry.

As I held Aster in my arms and walked around the room, Brian set in place the long, firm decorative bed pillows so as to barricade her from falling off. "Hi baby," I whispered into her ear. "So happy we're together." I kissed her head, and kissed it again. It was an amazing feeling to hold her close as we prepared for our first night together. I was still nervous, though, because I had never before slept in a bed with a baby. I hoped that I would even be able to sleep at all. Luckily, it seemed to me as if Aster was tired, because while I was holding her she rubbed her eyes and yawned a few times.

"This is good," I whispered to Brian. "Maybe she's ready to go to sleep."

I slid under the white sheet and Brian handed me the baby. I tried to rub her back, but she didn't seem to like it because she squirmed away from me. So I positioned myself close enough so I could feel her and tried to relax. Soon I dozed off. But every time this busy child wriggled about I woke up. She was asleep and moving around like nothing I had ever seen. I had trouble sleeping for more than a few minutes at a time because I was terrified that all that moving around would displace one of the pillows, and she would fall off the bed. Every time I nodded off and she moved even slightly, I jolted awake. This happened a dozen times or more before midnight when I realized I had to do something to get some sleep. I heard from other new mothers how scary it was to fall asleep next to their babies but nothing could have prepared me for this. Luckily my husband was with me.

I turned on the light and said to Brian, "Honey, she's too restless for me to relax, and we've both simply got to get some sleep."

I asked him if he would mind if I took an entire sleeping pill, but in order for me to feel okay with that we needed to put Aster in the crib. I carefully picked her up, and he helped me set her gently down. She was sleepy and seemed okay with the transition from bed to crib.

"It's hard to believe she slept with her nanny, isn't it?" I said.

"Well, she doesn't know us at all, really."

"That's true."

We covered her loosely with a small fleece blanket a friend gave us before leaving New Mexico. She did not fuss, but for at least ten minutes or so still moved about before finally settling in.

"Thank God," I said, and swallowed the pill. "I'll see you in the morning."

My head crashed into the pillow and minutes later I was gone. Until an hour or two later when I heard through my groggy haze the faint cries of a baby, which soon registered as Aster in what must have been a full-blown night terror. I sat straight up. Half asleep I saw Brian cradling Aster in his arms as she cried and cried and cried.

"Let me put on some music," I said, and bounced out of bed to turn on the portable speaker that was attached to a CD player. I quickly thumbed through the selection I brought along and put on Kirtana, a musician who plays peaceful, spiritually uplifting songs that I thought might help soothe her. I then fixed a bottle as quickly as my neophyte mommy hands could. I instructed Brian on how to sit with her in his arms with her head tilted back as she sucked in the liquid until it was finished. She still whimpered, though, so Brian stood up again and moved about the room with her as the music lulled her back to peace.

Sitting up in bed bleary-eyed, I watched my husband and daughter in their very first bonding dance, an emotional sight for me to witness. Aster was nestled deep into his shoulder. And then it was I who was moved to tears. I watched as Brian comforted this frightened child in the depths of night, in a strange city where unfamiliar sounds could still be heard. It was after two in the morning, and the music played until Aster was in an indestructible sleep. He set her back down in the crib, and then lay down in his bed. I crept quietly over, and nestled myself into his very over-tired body.

"That was so beautiful," I said, and wiped my nose and eyes on my t-shirt. "I love you."

I went back to the other bed and turned off the light.

"I love you too," he said.

Morning arrived and Brian and I did not feel too rested. But, we were so glad to see that Aster was still sleeping. It was a blissful sight, our baby sound asleep in her own world. I crawled into bed with Brian for a while as he held me in his arms and we stared at our daughter.

"Wow," I whispered.

"Wow is right," he quietly agreed. "She's amazing."

I pushed myself up and turned to kiss Brian lightly and then crept out of the bed. I stepped close to the crib and peered in on her. I gently put my hand on her tiny little body, all snuggled in a fleece onesie we packed that was way too big. I felt her forehead, and boy was she hot.

"We're going to have to get creative tonight," I quietly said to Brian, "because this nightie isn't right for this climate. It could be snowing outside and she'd be warm. I don't know what I was thinking bringing winter wear."

"We did the best we could."

"Maybe."

Aster stirred then, and I froze. I didn't want to be the cause of her waking up because I was talking too loudly. She didn't wake up, though. But it seemed as if her breathing just got more obvious. I stood still listening for nearly a minute. And even though I didn't think we needed to get her to a hospital, I did feel that something would have to be done.

Trying not to worry, I mimed to Brian that I was going into the closet area to do some yoga. He got back into bed and put his head down on the pillow, as I quietly shut the heavy door and rolled out my travel yoga mat. After about fifteen minutes of stretching and breathing, and a short headstand, I slowly opened the door. Aster had moved to the other end of the crib, but her eyes were still shut. Brian too was resting.

I tiptoed to the table and fixed Aster her morning bottle. This precious little girl was so cute lying there. A pacifier hung limply from her mouth, staying in place because she had it smashed up against one of the crib bumpers. I sat on the edge of the bed as Brian got up and dressed for the day. I gazed at her, not quite believing that we were in Africa, that this was our daughter, and soon we would all be returning to the U.S.A. to start our life as a family. I did not carry this child inside of me, I thought, and saying that she is my daughter seemed too surreal to be true. But it soon would be true. I wanted to reach in and grab her, to squeeze her close and kiss her all over. But that would not be wise: for one, because I still didn't want to wake her up; and two, I didn't want to scare her. After all, I was still a stranger.

It was December 1, 2008: Embassy Day. We had been waiting for this monumental occasion for about a year. If all went well, today we would officially become a family. If all went the way it was supposed to, we would from here on celebrate December 1 as our *Gotcha Day*, a common name given for the day that families celebrate the anniversary of their child's adoption. While we might not ever really know the exact date of Aster's birth, we would always know and celebrate our family's "birth" date. I was so excited. I went over to Brian and sat down on the bed. As we held each other close, Aster made baby sounds. She was awake and we moved to the crib.

She looked up at Brian and then at me. I nudged him because after the connection those two had shared a few hours ago I thought it might be better for him to be the one to pick her up. We didn't want to startle her.

"Are you sure?" he tentatively asked.

"Absolutely."

Brian took his daughter in his arms and then kissed her on the top of the head.

"Love you, Aster," he said.

"We love you, little one."

I stayed close and lightly touched her back. She felt sweaty, poor thing.

"Put her down on the bed, honey, so I can get that thing off of her."

The phone rang then and I picked it up. Breakfast was to be served in fifteen minutes. I hadn't yet brushed my teeth or dressed, and we still needed to find something for Aster to wear. Yikes.

I told Brian to use the bathroom while I put some clothes on Aster, and I would wash up after he was done. But as soon as he started to shut the door, Aster began to cry. Uh-oh, I thought, this is not going to be easy.

"It's okay, little one, he's just going to the bathroom. He'll be right back."

No go. Aster would have nothing of it. Her crying grew louder as she made her wishes known: *Daddy no leave!*

"Better keep the door open," I said, and he looked at me as if I were nuts, but he did anyway. I sat with Aster on the edge of the bed and bounced her gently, as her crying quieted a little. I am sure that he hadn't foreseen using the toilet in front of his daughter, but duty called, so to speak, and he did what he had to do.

After just a few minutes, he took her back into his arms. She clung to his t-shirt as if the floor was on fire. She immediately stopped crying, and when I went in to brush my teeth she didn't fuss at all. At this time, her need for Brian and lack of desire for me was of little concern. Though I could tell that during the coming week I would be the one to do the errands out and about while he stayed at the guesthouse with Aster, at that early stage it did not bother me. I felt joy seeing how close she felt already to Brian and could tell by his expression and the gentle way in which he was able to soothe her that he too was being nurtured. Together they were quite a pair.

I dug out of the suitcase a simple outfit for Aster, and asked Brian to lay her on the bed again. I nearly forgot that we had not changed her diaper in, oh, about thirteen hours. During her night crying it hadn't occurred to me to do so. By now the diaper was soaked. When I removed it, I was flabbergasted to see the skin underneath. Patches of inflamed red tissue and bumps dominated the area. Though the night before I had seen signs of a diaper rash, it looked far worse now. Her hands went straight for the area, and she scratched at herself like a cat with fleas. Later I would admit how stupid and selfish it was of me to be so concerned about my sleep, because clearly if I hadn't taken the pill, or at least not a whole one, I might have been clear-headed enough to change the diaper. Even if the rash wasn't entirely my fault, I probably contributed to it somewhat and this made me feel like an idiot. Due to our fatigue, jetlag, and ignorance, this lack of attentiveness caused our daughter unnecessary pain.

"Oh, baby, wow, this does not look good at all. Watch her, please," I said to Brian as I rushed to the cosmetic bag and got out the calendula cream and cornstarch powder I had brought from the States. As gently as I could, I wiped her, sprinkled some powder on, and waved my hands across the area to try to dry it before putting on a new diaper. I dabbed some of the cream on the worst areas and hoped for the best.

Before we headed downstairs, I filled the diaper bag with what I might need at the breakfast table. Aster did not have a single tooth yet, so I was not certain how well we would be able to feed her solid food. I packed her a bottle and a teething biscuit.

A small young woman, maybe no more than sixteen, with a kind smile and a generous disposition, served breakfast that first morning and all the mornings to come. Her name was Almaz, and she wore a tattered but clean sweater that covered a worn t-shirt and a below-the-knee skirt. She was wearing this same outfit whenever we saw her. Her smile was genuine and ever-present. I tried not to feel sad when I saw her always in the same clothes. But her smile was contagious. I filed her image away to pull out as a future life lesson. She, along with many people I saw in Ethiopia, no matter what was going on, kept a smile on her face.

Each morning we had the option of an omelet or French toast. Each morning we chose the omelet, knowing protein we felt comfortable eating might be hard to come by the rest of the day. A pot of strong, instant coffee (what happened to the roasted beans from the coffee ceremony?) also graced the table, which Brian and I were relieved to see, as we were in dire need of our morning caffeine. Aster was strapped to Brian's body in the sling that held her against his beating heart. I sat in a chair next to them and felt relieved that our daughter's wide-eyed fascination with her surroundings showed she was doing okay. Our server asked if the baby would like some eggs. "I don't know," I looked at Brian. "What do you think?"

"Sure, why not?"

When a plate of plain scrambled eggs was set down in front of us, Brian spooned tiny bites into Aster's mouth. She rapidly gummed her way through the eggs, eating the entire plate within minutes, which on the one hand pleased me because she was so tiny and needed to put on weight. But it also concerned me, because if she was this hungry perhaps she had not been fed well while in the care of WAA.

GETTING READY TO GO OUT in public to head for the Embassy appointment was no easy task. Though I had selected outfits for Brian and me, for some strange reason, I did not pack proper clothes for Aster. Having been too worried about other essentials, like health and well-being while in Africa, and making sure we had all the necessary paperwork with us, I failed to bring anything appropriate for her to wear outside the guesthouse. The one item I did have, a white lace dress, was just too huge, not to mention I had nothing to put under it and it was too sheer to wear on its own. I now wonder why I even packed this dress. Because we knew that Ethiopia is an Orthodox Christian country and the dress code is conservative, we were concerned that being in public dressed too casually, baby or not, would be a sign of disrespect. Brian and I wanted to display to the Ethiopians we encountered that we understood their customs and would raise our daughter appropriately.

In my memory, the experience of getting Aster ready for the Embassy appointment that morning is a blur. I don't even remember if I was the one to dress her, or if Brian orchestrated it with me as the coach, which seems logical now because at that time she was still pushing me away. As far as I can recall, she seemed quite delighted to be playing dress-up as we tried on a few things. I picture the scene with her being patient and happy while we took our time figuring out what would be best. There was nothing that showed she felt any discomfort about being with us. She seemed like such an easy child already. Less than one day and all of the pre-adoption reading we did about how upset children can be was flying out the window.

As I reached one of her hands up and tried to slide an arm through one of the armholes, I got the giggles. "Oh my gosh," I said, and Aster looked me straight in the eyes. "Isn't your new mommy silly?" I'm not sure what she thought, but I was grateful my ineptness didn't cause her to fuss.

"What's so funny?" Brian said.

"I feel like I'm dressing a doll. I have no idea what I'm doing."

"You don't? How do you think I feel?"

"We should have been reading Dr. Spock," I said.

Brian chuckled. "No kidding. What were we thinking only reading adoption books? Look at us! We hardly know how to put on her socks!"

Several of the pieces of clothing that I mailed as a donation to the Addis care center were inside the bag Aster arrived with. Although too large, one of them would simply have to work. Without much to choose from, I decided on a faded green t-shirt dress with a New York Giants football team logo stitched on the front. Underneath I would get more creative and layer her in a far-too-big top with the sleeves rolled up. I found a pair of white tights and we both carefully pulled them up her tiny legs as she squirmed and giggled. And on her feet? Well, it would have to be something because going without shoes would be unacceptable even if she was not yet walking. A pair of Winnie-the-Pooh sneakers, albeit too big, would have to do.

Okay, so at least we did a good job making up for my boneheaded move of not bringing the appropriate clothes. But we were still on edge because we had no idea what we were going to be asked during our appointment.

"Weren't we supposed to have been given some information from Tefere before leaving?" I asked Brian.

"Try not to worry," he assured me, "we aren't there yet."

I did not feel informed enough about what to expect once we got to the Embassy. We still did not know everything we should about Aster's social history. If we failed to properly answer the questions we would be asked, there's no telling what would happen. It was possible, we heard, for some families not to make it through during this initial appointment, which would then require more paperwork to be filed. Just because we had the appointment and were headed to the American Embassy didn't mean that getting our daughter's visa to come home with us was a slam-dunk. I would have liked some reassurance from Tefere, but it looked like that wasn't going to happen.

At least the clothes thing was working out. Although faded, Aster's dress was clean and her hair was still done up very nicely. When we were called for our turn, we would make sure that her face was free of teething biscuit remnants and that her nose was wiped clean. Still, Brian and I were nervous. We had no reason to think there would be problems with our case, but we recalled the horror stories that prospective parents went through with missing papers in their file. As previously mentioned, some end up having to stay in Ethiopia much longer than planned.

The mini-van that WAA hired for the week pulled up to the curb outside the gate of the guesthouse. Ruth, a single African-American woman from northern California, met her two children just that morning, a brother and sister, eight and six years old. Dressed well, the three of them stood at the idling car without saying a word. They barely had any time to get to know each other before heading to the Embassy. The couple from Portland acted as if they had been with their baby boys for months already, even though it was just two days. Maybe it was because they had a five-year-old birth daughter back in the States that they appeared like old pros at this parenting thing. I made a mental note to watch them carefully and ask them the many questions that would arise over the next several days.

Stepping up and into the rickety van, Brian bumped his head on the low and torn interior roof. He grimaced, but did not make a sound. We got in first and squeezed our way into the back row. No seat belts. Springs coming up out of the seats. Windows open on this warm Ethiopian day, and when the driver got going, the smell of diesel fuel flooded the car. We tried not to breathe in too deeply.

The van parked at the curb across from the heavily guarded American Embassy. Nobody told the driver to let us off right in front so that we wouldn't have to maneuver our children across the street. This must have been quite a sight to see. With no crosswalks, medians, or stoplights in sight, attempting to get across the street was tricky. The traffic was thick and unrelenting and we did not have the right of way. As a white woman with a black child, I couldn't help thinking what Aurora had told us about being out in public, even though Tefere said that was a bunch of baloney. In actuality, Tefere seemed to be right. We didn't run into anybody who appeared to have a problem with us. Though we did get some funny looks here and there, nobody said anything. In fact, nobody seemed to notice us much at all, because even though we were a group of new parents carrying babies, it took several minutes for us to cross the street. It didn't seem to matter who we were; we were treated like everybody else with no pedestrian right of way.

Minimal, uninspiring landscaping lined the narrow walkway as we met up with Tefere, who arrived early in a separate car. We all followed him into the Embassy where, not unlike the Customs window at an airport, we approached a glass cage and handed over our passports. Easily cleared, we continued to follow our leader into a large, sparsely furnished waiting room. I remember the area as gray and cool, and nearly void of people. Besides the three families from our group, there was one other couple with a baby boy. Nobody could say how long the wait would be. I had to use the toilet, but I decided to hold it for a while because I did not want to miss our slot.

The father of the baby was bouncing him up and down and pacing the floor as the boy cried. I felt sorry for them but was relieved that Aster, snot and all, so far, didn't seem to be a crier. More than anything, our daughter appeared quite entertained. She was alert to all that was going on, seemingly filled with inquisitiveness. I thought about her diaper rash and the cold she was suffering and wondered how she could exhibit contentment in the midst of all that her body was going through. Brian and I smiled at each other, happy to see Aster so calm.

"What a big girl you are," I said to her. "Honey, let's get her out of the sling for a while. Give you a break."

I pulled from the diaper bag a disposable mat and spread it on the floor in front of two connecting chairs for Brian and me. Though a bit dingy, the entire room was clean enough, so I wasn't too worried. Then I undid the ties of the sling, lifted her out, and set her on the paper blanket. Brian and I sat within reach of Aster. I took out a rattle that played a tune, and a teething biscuit. She took the cookie, but ignored the toy, and I quickly retrieved some wipes in order to keep up with the mess. I was committed to keeping her clothes food-free until we were through with our appointment.

One family-to-be at a time, Tefere approached and pulled us individually aside. "Thank God," I said to Brian. "Finally he's going to tell us what to say."

"Better late than never, I guess."

We were second to meet with him and were really curious by the time our turn arrived. He handed Brian a small white paper with a list of some sort typed on it. Tefere told us that the paper contained the answers we were to give when the Embassy official asked specific questions: Half-orphan; Mother not living; Father unknown; Born in Wukro, Province Tigre; Date of Birth . . . 2007; Orphanage . . . WHOA! *Something is rotten in the state of Denmark.*

So he told us to say Aster's mother had died. This was news. At the time of the referral we were told that she was too ill and poor to care for her, not that she was dead. Did she pass away since then? And why weren't we told of this prior to five minutes away from our "test?" There was also a discrepancy about where Aster was born. The referral form reported Mekele, but now we were told she was born north of Mekele in a town called Wukro, located near the border of Eritrea. We were minutes away from being interviewed at a U.S. Embassy about our almost-daughter and all that mattered was responding the way we were told to. I didn't have time to question Tefere about why this information did not match what WAA had told us from the start. The only thing I could do was memorize what was on the slip of paper and recite it at the appropriate time so we could pass this Embassy exam and get the hell out of Dodge.

Another fifteen minutes later, and my bladder felt ready to burst. I read the slip of paper one more time and handed it back to Brian. "Should we put her back in the sling?" I asked before leaving.

"Probably a good idea."

Brian positioned the sling for its occupant. I picked up Aster from the floor, slipped her back in, and tied the ends tightly enough to support Brian's back. And then I dashed out of the waiting area to find my way into the ladies' room.

Aster's mother is dead, repeated in my mind like an unwelcome mantra. As I entered the bathroom, though, that news was knocked out of my head. It smelled horrible, the garbage cans were filled to the brim, no soap, and the mirrors were simple pieces of tin screwed into the cement wall. It sure didn't feel like I was inside a bathroom at a U.S. Embassy. Although it was functional enough, I had to breathe through my mouth. Not only did the décor of the room appear ignored, but something else very odd was going on: two women were in the corner as one of them pulled from inside of a black garbage bag traditional dresses and the other looked as though she were deciding which one to take. They didn't seem to mind the smell. Part of me wanted to ask if the makeshift boutique was open to the public so I could look through the selection. The rational side admitted that I did not have time. Besides, this was not a place I wanted to hang out any longer than absolutely necessary. I put the shopping out of my mind and sped into one of the cavernous stalls.

Aster's mother is dead. Someone has some explaining to do. Though it had long ago started to sink in that international adoption may not be as simple as filing some papers and flying to Africa, the reality of how seriously difficult it is was now staring me down. As I ran cold water over my hands and shook them dry over the sink, I realized that there is so much more going on than perhaps any adoptive parent would ever be privy to. But I didn't have time to think about that.

I rushed back to the waiting area wanting to review these new facts with Brian. When I returned, he and Tefere appeared animated; our names had been called and if I had not shown up in thirty seconds, they would have let somebody else go before us.

"Sorry," I said, as Tefere whisked us up a flight of stairs.

"How you doing, Aster?" Brian quietly cooed.

"Just a few minutes more, little one, and we're done."

Tefere guided us quickly to the window where we anxiously handed over our passports again. My armpits were wet, and my heart was beating fast. Aster was squirming in the sling. I wiped her nose, as whatever it was that her body was fighting continued to drain. But our little girl stayed quiet. She looked around, and I touched her head.

"We're here, baby girl," I whispered close to her ear. "We're almost a family."

I stood next to Brian shoulder-to-shoulder. We squeezed each other's hands and looked at each other with knowing, *we did it* sort of expressions. The light-haired young man behind the glass smiled as he looked at us and reviewed our paperwork. Brian rubbed the small of my back. I looked at him and smiled, and we both smiled at Aster. When Brian brushed a finger across her cheek she smiled back.

The answers on Tefere's paper matched exactly the questions the Embassy Man asked. Within one minute we were done. "Congratulations," he said and smiled again.

"That's it?" Brian asked.

"Congratulations," Tefere said and hugged us all. "You're officially a family."

Our faces lit up the dull waiting room as we sauntered back in and were greeted with hugs and congratulations from our companions. Tefere called for the next couple to join him, the folks from Portland, with the twin boys, and I sat back down in a relaxed heap of sublime completion. It was just a matter of days before we would be back home in Santa Fe. No more just husband and wife; we were now three. After that unexpectedly quick exchange with the official behind the glass window everything had forever changed. This was a moment to sip in, like a frozen drink on a hot summer day. I let the cool relief wash through me and nourish my parched mind. The months of stressful waiting, the reams of paperwork, wads of money, the reading and worrying and concerns over not packing the right stuff for the baby, or being able to find our way around Addis Ababa, wondering if we would pass our Embassy appointment ... all of these were things of the past. The present felt perfect. Our future loomed beautifully bright before us, as I continued to watch Brian and Aster, fitted seamlessly together, a vision I had longed to see, and will never forget.

There was still one large looming issue: even if Tefere's information was correct as far as the government was concerned, Brian and I did not know if it was true. There was something so odd about what just transpired. A corner of my mind reserved a space for the contradiction of supposed facts. The appointment went so smoothly that I felt ridiculous ever feeling concerned that it wouldn't. About Aster's birth mother? Like one of my favorite literary characters Scarlett O'Hara often says, "Oh fiddle-dee-dee, I'll worry about that tomorrow."

By the time all three families passed their appointments, it was time for supper. The celebratory nature inside the van provided an endorphin rush that our tired bodies needed to fuel us through the evening. Ruth's kids were laughing and gleeful, their smiles huge and contagious. Ruth was crying shyly as she held her children close, an arm around each one. The Portland-bound twins showed signs of the same nose gunk and difficulty breathing, so if their parents, the experts of the bunch, weren't going straight back to the guesthouse, we might as well not either. The group agreed to go with Tefere's restaurant suggestion, a place that catered to American digestive tracts.

Dim bulbs and candles lit the cave-like dining room. Aster was still in the baby sling, but before we sat down at a long table in the center of the room, I untied the wrap and she sat freely on Brian's lap. We all reviewed the menus, which were translated into English alongside the Amharic. Our dinner companions were more adventurous than we, ordering traditional Ethiopian dishes, including *injera*, a spongy, sour flatbread along with *wat*, or spicy stews, in which one dips the *injera*. Traditionally, Ethiopian cuisine is eaten with the right hand, but boring old me used utensils to spoon in some vegetable soup and rice, which I was able to help Aster eat as well. Brian joined in keeping it simple, and also just ordered soup and rice, though when the other foods arrived and we were offered tastes, he tried the spicier fare. Even though we didn't want to drink juice or soda, as they were likely prepared with tap water, they served alcohol at this restaurant. Tired as we were, we decided to celebrate with one of the featured Ethiopian beers. The others joined in trying the beer, and when it was served, we all raised our glasses.

"Here's to our kids," Ruth said.

"Cheers!"

"We did it!"

Tefere joined in. "Congratulations, everybody. What a wonderful day this has been."

The older kids wandered about the table. They both visited Aster, wanting to engage her. She would have nothing to do with them, though, turning her head in toward Brian's chest. The kids seemed a bit sad over the baby's rejection, but the sight of Aster snuggled on Brian's lap pushing her head into his chest was heartwarming.

By the time we were back in the van making our way slowly through the thick traffic to the guesthouse, the sun had set. Our driver seemed to enjoy the local sport of honking, using his hand on the horn to do the talking. The streets of Addis Ababa remained filled. And even though we were still on a high of sorts after our celebratory meal, it was hard not to let the poverty get in the way. Whenever we were stalled or stopped, bone-thin people in shredded clothes, looking unhealthy and hungry with babies wrapped around their bodies, tapped on the windows of the car, motioning with their hand to their mouth. The van became a magnet for beggars who saw our faces through the window. I felt the reality of this place seep into me deeper and deeper. I remained silent the rest of the way back as I prayed for each person I saw. *May the power of God protect you ... the love of God enfold you.*

It had been another very long day, and I was ready for bed.

As OUR FIRST DAY AS a family came to a close, Aster's discomfort from her diaper rash increased. Even though we changed her diaper every two hours, the rash seemed to progress throughout the day. The poor child was crying and scratching with a vengeance. Though we thought we came prepared with powder and cream, it wasn't nearly enough to stop her from being in such discomfort. After I removed her diaper, I decided it would be best not to put one back on for a while. And though Brian at first was super-conscious about her urinating on the guesthouse linens, it was not hard to convince him how important it was to let the infected area go without a diaper for a while. I berated myself for not using more space in the luggage for a week's worth of chlorine-free, unscented diapers because she was going through a dozen a day, and I only brought enough for a half-day more. I was angry with myself, but I didn't have time for regrets. Tomorrow I would find my way to a market and do my best to buy less irritating diapers, but right now we needed to get her a prescription-strength cream of some sort, and we needed it before morning.

I called downstairs and asked the attendant at the front desk to please call Tefere and have him call us back. Brian wrapped the baby's bottom half loosely in a towel as I waited for the telephone to ring. When Tefere called, I told him we needed his help. He said he would rush to the all-night pharmacy to buy some cortisone cream because that was pretty much all we could do. Forty-five minutes later, he knocked on our door. By then she had calmed down a bit. We thanked Tefere, paid him back what he spent, and carefully rubbed some hydrocortisone cream onto the inflamed skin. After reluctantly putting on another diaper, I prepared a bottle and handed it to Brian. When she devoured the formula, he was able to set her into the crib, where she fell into a deep sleep.

BRIAN AND I SPENT THE last day in Addis Ababa preparing for our evening flight back to the United States. One of the services we enjoyed that week was paying a small fee to have our clothes laundered. Each piece was hand-washed and line-dried by one of the guesthouse staff, and even though some of our white items came back varying shades of blue, I was not annoyed; we had more clothes than we would ever need. Brian and I acknowledged that compared with nearly everybody with whom we came in contact in Ethiopia, we had it made.

In addition to tipping each of the employees at the guesthouse, Brian and I decided that we would give as much of our belongings away as we could. We agreed to pack only what we needed for the flight home. This left at least one item for each of the eight or so staff that had graciously attended to our every comfort that week in Africa.

When Brian handed Selassie a near-new Eddie Bauer button-down, the man cried. Then he did something astonishing: he asked if he could speak with me out in the courtyard a bit later. During the few days that we had known him, he made it abundantly clear how desperately he needed financial assistance. I never did figure out what his exact role was at the guesthouse, and several times I saw him engaged with a salaried employee in what looked like an uneasy conversation.

A little while after we had given him the shirt, I went downstairs and there he was. He jumped up from the couch and eagerly approached me, motioning for me to come out into the courtyard with him. Once outside, he directed me to sit in the one plastic chair that was out there. Selassie knelt down in front of me. His head was down, and when he looked up tears were streaming down his face. He spoke in broken English with a thick accent while pulling something out of his jacket pocket.

"This is a picture of me," he said and handed me a surprising photograph. Selassie looked dressed for a prom. It was a staged photo, with a kitschy backdrop, and he was in a suit with a flower at his lapel. I looked at the image and then back up to him. Hardly recognizable as the same young man.

"Wow," I said. "You look great."

"Thank you." Selassie smiled and proceeded to tell me about his mother in Gondar, the historical city where he was born, far north of Addis Ababa. His mother was ill, he explained, and he needed money to pay for hospital bills. But the work was not coming. He went on to whine that he wanted to go to school and soon the tuition would be due. He put his head back down and asked if we would be able to help him with some money.

In an instant I had gone from feeling deeply sad for Selassie and his situation to feeling manipulated and angry back to feeling genuine pity. Even if he did not help us just to help us, if he all along harbored an agenda, perhaps preying on me because I come off as an American softy, still, he was obviously in a world of hurt. But, I had no idea if he gave this line to every tourist who would listen. We tipped him as we did the others and though he said he couldn't find a job, I didn't perceive him in any more need than anybody else. I did not know how to respond. Mostly in that moment I didn't want to make a scene.

"I'm sure we can give you some money," I told him.

Selassie took my hands in his and kissed them. I felt silly and sad and used.

I went back upstairs and discussed Selassie's request with Brian. There remained only a few hours before we would head for the airport and a rush of emotion ran through us. We decided to give him five hundred birr, which equals about $35. While Aster was napping in Brian's arms I took the cash downstairs where he was waiting. I led him aside and handed him the money. Selam, the young woman at the front desk, saw the exchange and made a *tsk-tsk* sound, as she lowered her eyes and shook her head from side to side in obvious disapproval. I am fairly certain that Selam wanted me to notice her, which made me feel particularly uncomfortable. She saw me give Selassie more money than we had given her, which embarrassed me. She certainly had gone out of her way to help us out, too. Even though five hundred birr hardly dented our bank account, we didn't have enough cash to give more to the others.

With very little time left before we would leave Africa, Brian and I continued donating our giveaways to the staff.

I piled up t-shirts, pants, two of Brian's button-downs, two sweaters and a pashmina. I put the items in a cloth bag, and every time I heard an employee outside our room, a housekeeper, clothes washer, or handyperson, I opened the door and smiled, pulled out an appropriate offering and handed it to that person. There were two people working downstairs I wanted to include, but decided to wait until we were just about to leave to give them their items.

After picking through the entire contents of our suitcase, most of which were easily replaceable, I decided to distribute the few pieces of jewelry I wore. Silver hoop earrings, some bangle bracelets, and a silver ring I found on the beach when I lived in San Diego. There was one item, though, that I debated about giving away. The mother of a dear friend who had died of cancer a few years back gave it to me. It was a silver angel on a long chain, which I did not take off the entire trip except to go through airport security. I didn't have much time to weigh the pros and cons of leaving this memento behind. The deciding factor was that Selam had been so kind to Aster and us. I wanted to let her know that we were grateful to her. I wanted her to realize, through this gesture, that she made a difference in this world. As far as the gift, I knew that I would miss it, but my desire to make Selam happy was stronger than my wish to hold onto it. I believed that my friend would approve of me giving it to her. There were times after he passed away that I felt his presence near me, like a guardian angel of sorts. It seemed fitting now to give the angel a new owner.

At four o'clock, the room phone rang. It was Tefere, and the taxi was waiting to take us to the airport. Since the others were leaving a day later, we were the only ones of the group to go at this time. We said our goodbyes to the other families at breakfast so now were focused on not forgetting anything.

Downstairs, I motioned to the guard, miming *heavy bags*, and said, "Please." Aster was a barnacle stuck to Brian so he couldn't carry the suitcases down the two flights. The guard understood and followed me back up. Once inside I realized I had not saved any clothes for him. As I scanned the bathroom, checking to make sure we weren't leaving anything crucial behind, with some embarrassment, I offered him the remainder of the toiletries that were sitting out. I was relieved to see his excitement.

"What is this?" he asked. I explained the purpose of shower gel, and how to open a perfume sample. "Oh, my wife be so happy," he said. There was just a smidgen of perfume remaining in the slender vial that a saleswoman had thrown into my shopping bag at a cosmetic store in Santa Fe where I sometimes buy face cream. My heart hurt when he responded with such gratitude for my leftovers.

I rushed back down the stairs behind the guard, and there stood Selassie next to Brian and Aster. His face lit up when he saw me. Brian's expression was one of disbelief and resolve. He shrugged his shoulders.

Before acknowledging Selassie, I crossed over to Selam. She smiled without showing her teeth, in the shy way that I had grown accustomed to over the past week. She looked me straight in the eyes, and told me, "You are so beautiful. I am going to miss you here."

"You have been very good to us, Selam. Thank you for everything." She held her gaze and I started to feel sad, which was something I did not expect or want to feel at that moment. I took the necklace from around my neck and draped it over her head. "This is for you," I said.

Her eyes filled with tears, and she hugged me. "Thank you," she said as she pulled away. She grinned wide enough now for me to see all of her bright teeth.

I kissed her on both cheeks, and left her side. Brian was still with Selassie, but had been inching towards the courtyard.

When I met up with them, Selassie said, "I have a gift for you. How much room you have in your suitcase?" Underneath Selassie's arm was something large and thin wrapped in white paper.

"A bit," I said.

He handed the gift to me and I took it. Underneath the paper was a typical wall hanging souvenir, the kind I saw on my few trips outside the guesthouse. A country boy was depicted standing with a long loaf of bread, drawn in a rough image and bound on wood with leather stripping.

"Thank you," Brian and I said. "You really shouldn't have."

I quickly wrapped it back up, and rushed into the courtyard to ask the guard if he would take out the largest suitcase from the trunk of the taxi. I unzipped it, laid the artwork on top, zipped the bag back up, and the guard put it back in the car.

I went back into the guesthouse where Brian and Aster were standing. Brian was saying his goodbyes to the staff and Selassie was hanging around with an eager, somewhat desperate expression.

"I'm going to meet you at the airport," Selassie said as we headed back outside.

When I said that it would be better for us to say goodbye to each other at the guesthouse, he looked dejected. Then he pulled a card out of his back pocket. I quickly opened it. It was a Hallmark type of thank you card with a wallet-size photo of him inside. He had written his email address on it, which seemed strange to me. Without thinking, Brian reciprocated and gave Selassie one of his art postcards, which had his email address on it.

"Please write to me," he said. "You are my family now."

I assured him that we would, but felt lousy telling him what I knew would probably end up being a lie. We were parents now, and I wasn't sure I would have much time to email even my closest friends.

On the taxi ride to the airport I felt relieved. Soon we would be on that long journey back to Santa Fe. Even if someday we hoped to return with our daughter so that she could come to know the country of her birth, for now, our mission was complete.

"Thank you, Ethiopia," I quietly said out loud. I held Brian's hand and turned my head to kiss him. "I love you," I said.

"I love you too."

I put my hand on Aster's back as she stayed cuddled in the sling next to her daddy's chest. "I love you, Aster. Love you, my daughter."

The feelings that pulsed through me in that taxi were many. So excited to be going home, so much love for this precious child next to me, so much respect and gratitude for a husband I felt honored to be mine. A sadness also remained, though, as the sun left a fiery glow across the sky.

We were leaving Ethiopia. Leaving Africa, with no idea when we would be back.

When we arrived at the airport, we had three hours to wait before boarding. We wanted to get there far ahead of time in order to be eligible for the first-come, first-served inexpensive upgrade to business class. It didn't matter to us where in Addis Ababa we waited until it was time for the plane to take off, except that when we got to the airport we realized we had to stand in line without chairs until they opened the ticket line.

About an hour later, after we were approved for business class and given temporary boarding passes, I was instructed to take the vouchers to a cashier where, after paying the fee, we would get our tickets. I waited in another line and took a deep breath. After a few minutes, I looked across the way at my husband, who carefully supported Aster's bottom with his hands. Standing on the hard, gray floor took its toll quickly. But we saw the end of our yearlong tunnel approaching, even if at a snail's pace.

Aster was tucked like a kangaroo baby next to her daddy. His shoulders were hunched over from the weight of her, having carried her on his body for more than an hour without break. He looked exhausted yet content. Already, I couldn't wait to be with them again. Was that really my daughter over there tied to my husband? Were those two actually my very own family? A deep feeling of contentment came over me in a way I never imagined possible.

"So sorry," the man behind the glass window said into his microphone. "Computer is down."

I shifted my weight and set my chin in my hand, elbow resting on the ledge. An older man that I recognized from the ticket line came up to wait behind me. He had left the side of an older woman dressed impeccably in traditional Ethiopian clothes: an ankle-length dress precisely wrapped around her body, with a matching shawl draped over her head and shoulders. She stood waiting near Brian and Aster.

"Did you and your husband adopt that baby?" he asked, pointing with his eyes. He looked like a local, but his accent did not sound like anything I had heard all week.

"Um, yes," I hesitantly said, not knowing what this gentleman might think of that. But my caution was uncalled for. The man bowed to me, took my hand, and kissed it.

"God bless you, my dear," he said. "I was born right here in Addis Ababa, and that is my mother who now lives in Virginia. I am a citizen of the United States of America, may God bless America. My mother only has residency, so I bring her back here once a year to visit. Ethiopia is not a good place for a child to grow up. God bless you. You and your husband are angels," he said and kissed my hand again.

The week had worn me out beyond measure and we still had nearly two days' worth of travel to get back home. When this man spoke with such generosity of spirit I felt covered in a healing salve. Knowing that an Ethiopian-American man appreciated that we were giving one child from his homeland an opportunity to grow up outside of poverty was an exclamation point at the end of our story.

"Thank you for saying so," I said to him. "But I have a very strong feeling that this beautiful child is the real angel here."

"What is her name?"

"Aster."

"Ah, yes, Aster."

I looked at my husband, who was looking at me with curiosity. I smiled, gave him the thumbs up, and turned around. The computer was back on. It was time to get our tickets and head for home.

EPILOGUE

TRANSITIONING TO PARENTHOOD AND UPDATE ON ETHIOPIA ADOPTION

July 2010. We have been home from Ethiopia for about twenty months. That first year was a tough one, and I think I speak for many adoptive moms when I say I often felt more like a nanny than a mother. But things have shifted. Aster and I are together now in a way I never dreamed possible. Thoughts enter my mind, and she voices them in Asterspeak. When I look at her in that very present way one often does while in nature, I tear up. I see in her eyes and feel in her embrace lifetimes of togetherness. My journey to motherhood was unexpected. My life has become a painting that explodes in vibrant colors before my very eyes.

"Motherhood is messy in so many more ways than I expected. A chaos of emotions and laundry. A life without boundaries, splitting at the seams and spilling over everywhere."

—From *Sing Them Home*, by Stephanie Kallos

This child of light entered my heart and forever has changed the way I do life.

To articulate the respect I feel for our destined connection has been a challenge. Sometimes I share my deepest, most sacred internal experience with others. Most of the time I don't. What I want most to convey is the deep satisfaction I feel having not given birth. This choice, seemingly having been made for me by circumstances outside of my control, in actuality now appears preordained. I am the mother of a person who did not grow in my womb, and this truth satisfies me to the core. The odd thing about this choice is that I now feel as if the clichéd cravings of a hormonal young woman only surfaced as a societal idea. I now feel it is truthful to say that I never craved the experience of raising a child that came from my DNA. I believe that my soul needed to meet up with this other soul that has nothing to do with me in this particular body, in this particular lifetime. I was meant to call Aster *daughter* as sure as she was meant to call me *mommy*. There is no other human being who could qualify herself in this role.

When I first became Aster's mother, I fantasized that hers was the spirit that I years ago had aborted. Today, this thought does not enter my mind; I do not need an explanation. There is something quite astonishing watching this *other* grow into herself, knowing that her blood did not come from me. I stand back more as an observer, a guardian, and only sometimes a guide. I do not feel attached in a way that would make me want to steer her life in a direction of my own making. She may not take to dance, as I once assumed a daughter would. She exhibits a love of extreme movement, running fast and hard, climbing high without fear. It delights me watching her be so herself. And there is relief too, witnessing her be so not like me. I know it is my job now to keep her this way, to guard her separateness as if it were a treasure owned by the queen. And I, her lady-in-waiting, must watch over the jewels to ensure nobody steals them.

I began to think about Aster's birth mother long before the nanny handed her to me. It took many months for my daughter's biological mother not to enter into my daily thoughts. I felt such deep sadness for this child who, we were told, would never have the opportunity to know the woman who birthed her. She supposedly had no other blood relatives, so seeking out her birth family would never be an option for Aster. Ours has been a long and unplanned but methodical process that took many odd twists and turns, and in the end proved that not everything you believe to be the truth really is. Though at times ignorance can be bliss, this has never been my motto, nor has it proven to be true. Knowing *what is* gives me the opportunity to make my own choices: I can choose to accept what I know to be true and deal with the sadness, fear, or anger, or I can bury my head in my hands and pretend I do not see. Most of my life I have wished I were the type who could live blind. But that has not been my destiny. For better or worse, I have always wanted to know the truth.

About five months after we returned, we needed to finalize Aster's adoption in the United States. In part, this meant getting her a birth certificate in the state of New Mexico. Because at the time of her referral, as mentioned in an earlier chapter, we had not been given a date of birth for her, I decided to check just one more time with our agency. I still had not gotten past the communication discrepancies that began at the time of our referral that only specified a birth month, but no date. No last name. No living relatives. How could this be if she were not one of the orphans supposedly found in a box picked up by the police, a story often given as the child's "social history"? At one point our agency said that Aster had been handed over by one of her birth mother's neighbors. If this were indeed the truth, then somewhere, somebody had lied; I never accepted how little information we were given. From current research I now know that the story we were told is common: mother too sick and/or poor, father "unknown." Before Aster became a legal citizen of the United States of America, I needed to let my concerns go. I could not afford to irritate the wrong person for fear, I thought, that our adoption would for some ridiculous excuse be halted.

As I wrote about earlier, a few weeks prior to leaving for Ethiopia I needed a birth date so we could apply for Aster's health insurance. Because we had none we made one up. Then, out of the blue, just about ten days prior to our departure, in a one-line email, Aurora wrote that Aster did indeed have a birth date in November and further stated that it was her birth mother who had said as much. When I phoned Aurora I asked in an incredulous tone how suddenly, after so little information from the very start, she could know the exact date of our daughter's birth? More than six months after she had given her baby girl up for adoption she was obviously still alive and well enough to tell somebody what day she gave birth to Aster. Aurora curtly told me that some undisclosed person in their Mekele care center had told them, "I know Aster. She was born … "

How, after nearly six months of no communication, did Aster's birth mother mysteriously surface? I just could not get past the strange manner in which this vital information had been conveyed. But again, I ignored it. I promised myself that I would deal with this odd news after we returned with our daughter, safe and sound in the United States.

Several months after returning from Africa, as we prepared to get Aster a New Mexico birth certificate I contacted the current agency director. I shared with him what our rep had told us about Aster's birth date, and because we needed something official for our adoption attorney to present to the court, I asked him to please send us something on his letterhead. This was vital because according to other records, her Ethiopian visa for example, her date of birth was the one we had made up. You can't just pick a birth date out of your pocket if indeed there is a real date available. We needed to know for sure. Aster had a right to know. Brian and I both felt strongly that it would eventually be important for her to know the day she was born, if indeed that information was available. I would never be able to forgive myself for not trying as hard as I possibly could to get her what I believed she needed: to know the day she was born. Everybody has a right to know this simple fact.

Naturally, we had been told that Ethiopia is a developing country, and when babies are born, mostly not in a hospital, there is no recording of this information. The orphanage nanny likely creates any date that is given to an adoptive parent. I had accepted this in the beginning. The made-up date is the one we had written on the *Child Referral Acceptance Form*, and this is why the Ethiopian government used it to finalize her adoption in that country. But when our rep emailed me an actual date, I pasted the email into Aster's Lifebook. To me, and one day to her, this would make it real enough. That would be the date that we would annually celebrate as her day of birth. And I would deal with other records back in the States upon our return.

When I contacted our agency director requesting he send us something official regarding Aster's birth date to give to our attorney, I received a few strongly worded emails indicating that whatever our representative had written us was wrong. One of his emails explained that when he had confronted our rep about our request, she denied ever having sent us the email with Aster's birth date, "as per her mother." Of course I had the original pasted in Aster's Lifebook, which I easily copied and mailed to both of them. Then, furious and frustrated as I was, I let the whole thing go.

We decided then that because there was so much seeming deceit and confusion surrounding Aster's birth that we would make her birthday the most useful date for her, one that would allow her to enter school at five, and not six. She was exhibiting advanced fine and gross motor skills for her supposed age, so our attorney told us that we should consult her pediatrician to get an approval to change her birth date from that which was written on her Ethiopian birth certificate. She would speak with the judge and state the facts that often no birth records are kept in Ethiopia, and often dates are made up just to satisfy the legal aspects of adopting an orphan into another country. Aster's doctor agreed that she could have been born earlier. Even if the height and weight charts would deem her in a low percentile according to U.S. standards, there was enough other evidence for her to "approve" an August birth date.

One of Aster's foster sisters was adopted into a home in the Northeast shortly before Aster's second birthday. I had become close with her adoptive mom because we used the same agency and had been communicating regularly. She is a social worker with grown kids. Her adopted teenage Ethiopian daughter barely made it out of Africa, due to her age, but thanks to the determination of her new mom, she is now a U.S. citizen.

Shortly after she arrived, I phoned to say hello and to thank her for the gifts that she had carried all the way from Mekele and mailed to us. Aster's nannies had asked this young woman to send Aster a traditional Ethiopian skirt and matching top and make sure we knew it was from them. This gesture touched me deeply, as it showed how Aster had been cared for; she hadn't just been a nameless child in some mass orphanage. I told Aster's foster sister that we were about to celebrate Aster's second birthday, even though we made up the date because we were never actually told the date she was born.

"Oh, would you like me to ask her mother?" she said.

This innocent, generous question opened a door that had been locked shut since the very beginning of our connection with Aster. I was stunned speechless. Until I replied, "Aster's mother is alive? What do you mean?"

"Yes of course, I know her."

Shortly after this conversation, summer 2009, stories such as this began to flood the blogs and Ethiopian chat groups online. Countless adoptive parents of Ethiopian children are discovering that the circumstances surrounding their child/children's adoption were false. Now, in mid-2010, the non–Hague-accredited country of Ethiopia may soon find that adoptions to parents living in Hague countries will no longer be possible. A plethora of solidly investigated reports tell of older children who, once they acquire the language to speak, share with their adoptive parents that they have a parent (or two), siblings, and other extended family living back home in Ethiopia.

A report in late December 2009 from Australian ABC TV's *Foreign Correspondent* indicated that the Australian government had been alerted to some not-so-transparent adoption practices in Ethiopia and they suspended all adoptions from that country. This news report exposed some serious trouble going on in the Ethiopian adoption system. The report disclosed the government's fear that children were being plucked from their birth families, and some mothers claimed they were tricked into giving up their children. A few months later this same news outlet reported that some children labeled "orphan" in actuality have families. Further, some were being advertised, so to speak, to adoptive families as being years younger than they actually were.

News reports like this widely publicized Australian one are becoming quite common. The fact is that in 2010 Ethiopia still has not signed the Hague Convention on intercountry adoption, yet hosts numerous adoption agencies that are Hague accredited and claim to have a high standard of practice. Even though this is a political issue, I choose to pose this question: Why is the Hague-accredited United States even allowing adoptions from countries that have not ratified the Hague Convention? Had I known then what I know now I cannot say that I would have taken the same path to our adoption. Ironically, however, the only reason I do know what I know is because of the path we took.

It is heartbreaking to think that the orphans of Ethiopia, having lost either one or both of their parents, may soon no longer have the opportunity to be adopted into families that will love and support them as they grow into healthy and well-adjusted Americans of Ethiopian descent. It is my hunch that the Ethiopian adoption program will not be in operation much longer. The United States needs to consider halting adoptions from Ethiopia, even if temporarily, as Australia did, until its government can take the time to enter into the Hague Convention on intercountry adoption and start a relationship with accredited countries that are committed to "prevent the abduction, the sale of, or traffic in children" for international adoptions.

I do, however, feel hopeful knowing that in July 2010 Secretary of State Hillary Clinton created a new foreign policy position at the U.S. State Department's Office of Children's Issues to focus on intercountry adoption and international parental child abduction. It is so exciting to realize that she appointed Ambassador Susan S. Jacobs as the Special Advisor of Children's Issues and that on January 24, 2011, Ambassador Jacobs invited the public to attend—via teleconference—a forum on Ethiopia adoptions called Solutions into Action. The proposed agenda included this question: "How do we move forward to ethically and transparently protect children, birth families and adoptive parents in Ethiopia?"

A phone number and access code were listed on the State Department's website, providing an opportunity for all interested to join the discussion. Not only were "civilians," such as myself, allowed to listen in and ask questions via an intermediary, but representatives from government agencies, UNICEF, adoption service providers and NGOs were also present.

To me, this felt like the first step in making international adoption a more transparent endeavor. The information presented was often quite candid and reassuring, in that I discovered that the concerns that I and countless other adoptive and prospective adoptive parents of Ethiopian children harbor are shared and being taking seriously by every person in all aspects of the process. The Ethiopian government, American employees at the embassy in Addis Ababa, adoption care providers and adoption agencies—many of those involved now seem to be on the same page.

Because at the start of this meeting it was announced that "this is off the record," and that the minutes would be posted on the State Department's website, I will let you, the reader, do your own research. The reason for adding this information to the Epilogue here is to share with you that transparency, honesty, and ethics have, even if perhaps only recently, become a great concern to those who have the power to oversee these adoptions. The meeting was enlightening and encouraging. For those who are interested, please keep this website bookmarked and check regularly for updates: http://adoption.state.gov/news/ethiopia.html.

After I learned that Aster's birth mother was in fact *not* deceased, I, understandably, was livid. Once again, I became obsessed with uncovering the lies that we had been told in order for this adoption to happen with as little work as possible on the part of our adoption agency. Because the director of our agency refused to acknowledge my discovery, I went to the teen's adoptive mom, who without hesitation gave me email addresses for employees of the Mekele orphanage. It wasn't long before I heard back the startling, yet wonderful news, that not only was Aster's birth mother alive, but Aster also has a half-sister, several uncles and an aunt. There still was no certain birth date, but at this point, that information seemed less vital than knowing our daughter had living blood relatives.

One day when the time comes, years from now, we will be able to provide Aster with the information that every adopted child should be privy to: a family name, and the names of family members to go with it. One day, before Aster becomes a teen herself, we will offer her the opportunity to visit her country of origin. We will take her to the place where she was born, and, if she wishes, help her meet the people who share her DNA.

What saddens me the most about international adoption is that transparency is not a given. It is my life's work, perhaps, to encourage openness between adoption agency and adoptive parents, between those who "rescue" the children from a life of poverty, and those who take money to do so.

So as not to end this account of my adoption story on a negative note, I will say this: I love you, Aster. You are my best girl ever, and if and when you do read this, please know that you have lived inside my heart for lifetimes. There is no turning back now. You are my daughter. I am your mommy. And I thank you for being so filled with light. In the end, you need to know, it is you who saved me.

OVERPOPULATION, THE ENVIRONMENT, AND CHOOSING ADOPTION

My intention with this appendix and its discussion of overpopulation as it relates to choosing to adopt over choosing to give birth is not to alienate women who have a strong bio-motherhood urge. As mentioned at the end of Chapter One, not giving birth in this lifetime did have something to do with the way that Brian and I felt, and still feel, about our suffering planet. We did not want to contribute to the environmental problem by adding yet another human. Fifteen years ago, when I was pregnant, having an abortion was not my idea. Even though at the time the decision had nothing to do with how I now feel about overpopulation, I accept having gone through with it, and appreciate not having added another human being to the planet.

If there are those out there who are as ambivalent about procreating as my husband and I were, you may find this section somewhat illuminating.

DRIVING A CAR IN OUR culture is not a right, it's a privilege, and there are strict laws governing how and who is given this right. Why then do we, as a society, support the right for adults to have as many children as they want? These are legitimate topics to debate, ideas that are in alignment with all of our children's future, and they should be acceptable to discuss. Though many people do not feel safe talking about overpopulation, nonetheless it is a subject that must be looked at.

I will admit that it is possible I feel comfortable with this discussion because I actually now have no possibility of ever giving birth. I cannot predict how I would have reacted to somebody else presenting this issue if instead I had been fertile, or even had been the birth mother of a child or two or three. Would I take my comments as a personal attack on my desire to give birth? I do not know. What I do know is that I have always been concerned about garbage, pollution, recycling, traffic, and poverty. Though I have too often turned a blind eye to social issues, simply because I never felt capable of making change, I have rarely held my tongue when I felt it was right to speak up. In the case of this particular book I cannot *not* mention overpopulation and how, when seriously explored, it must factor into a decision when a man or a woman wants to grow a family. I have placed this discourse in an appendix so as not to disrupt the flow of my personal story, and to allow those who wish to explore the topic the option to do so.

THOUGH CONTROVERSIAL NEWS ANCHOR LOU Dobbs is no longer hosting his nightly CNN show, on August 21, 2008, Dobbs facilitated a discussion on his evening news show about the United States' "population explosion." He asked one panel member, Robert Engelman of the Worldwatch Institute, "At a time when this country is being criticized for consuming so much of the world's resources, at a time when we are finding ourselves running into limits in terms of this country's resources, whether it be for building, production, whatever it may be, what is the environmental impact?"

"Demand matters," Engelman said. "We're starting to lose confidence that I think we used to have that we can always find more of everything we might need so it doesn't matter how many people are consuming. It clearly does matter, and what we're seeing in America is a high-consuming country that ... is going to be consuming more living space [and] more transportation."

Outraged, he questioned Engelman about the environmentalists. Where are they, he wanted to know, because the impact on the environment, the water supplies, even the air, is "tremendous." Dobbs wanted to know, as do I, why there is no discussion from this group of activists on what is a "critically important issue."

Engelman explained that the whole topic of overpopulation has become a very sensitive and scary area "for the environmental movement, as a movement, to take on."

Dobbs did not let this feeble excuse go, however, and explained that on his show an honest conversation, not a politically correct discussion, is valued. He continued to express his bafflement over why the topic of overpopulation is "scary." Engelman mentioned the possibility of abortion and immigration as sensitive areas, and people, he insisted, don't want to go there.

I must interpret him to mean that it's easier to just avoid this bio-ethical debate altogether rather than to have discussions about topics related to forced sterilization, or countries that place limits on the number of children people are allowed to conceive.

"How in the world is this planet going to support over nine billion people in the next four decades?" Dobbs asked into the camera.

What a question! Especially when his panel of experts explained that this projection is actually on the low side.

Some people will call me radical, and I will risk being labeled thusly. It is my job as the writer of this particular book to at least offer up some of the recent data that I discovered while exploring the topic of overpopulation. If I can touch just one person, change the course of one family tree to include an adopted child, rather than giving birth one more time, then I have done my job. And, if you are struggling with fertility problems and need a reason to feel really good about adoption without the sense of loss of your bio-motherhood, you can feel like you are doing something positive to help our planet too.

Overpopulation: The population of an environment by a particular species in excess of the environment's carrying capacity. The effects of overpopulation can include the depletion of resources, environmental deterioration, and the prevalence of famine and disease. Origin of word: 1802.

Unlike plagues of the dark ages or contemporary diseases we do not understand, the modern plague of overpopulation is soluble by means we have discovered and with resources we possess. What is lacking is not sufficient knowledge of the solution but universal consciousness of the gravity of the problem and education of the billions who are its victim.

—*Martin Luther King, Jr.*

According to Oxford University–educated Michael S. Teitelbaum, a demographer and Vice President at the Alfred P. Sloan Foundation in New York City, it is time for the United States "to recapture its leadership role on population issues; a continuation of this self-inflicted blindness to demographic insights is increasingly dangerous for U.S. foreign policy" (*Foreign Affairs* [Winter 1992–1993]).

It is now 2010, and population control has somehow taken on the status of an Orwellian concept. We are living in the era of evangelical radicalism, where both seemingly educated women and men spend countless hours orating about and attempting to overthrow Roe v. Wade, "the 1973 Supreme Court decision overturning a Texas interpretation of abortion law and making abortion legal in the United States."[7] The extreme amount of energy that continues to be expended in attempts to control a woman's body has swept the global crisis of overpopulation so far under the rug it no longer is recognized as an issue.

There are many ways to define overpopulation, and many places in the world that are overpopulated by any defini-tion …We are unwilling to say that in public.

We don't know a constructive way to suggest that there are too many of us … And so we attribute deaths from lung disease in Los Angeles to air pollution and deaths from hunger in Bangladesh to a storm.…

*The subject of population stirs up the ethnic hatreds of
the world, the resentment of the poor, the guilt of the rich …
We would rather say it was a storm that killed those
helpless people in Bangladesh. Or that it was the poverty
of the Bangladeshis. We would prefer not to think that it
was our own silence.[8]*

On July 18, 2008, *USA Today* reported that provisional data
released by the National Center for Health Statistics revealed
that the year 2007 saw a record number of babies born in
the United States. These 4,315,000 new human beings did
not come, at the time of this report, with statistical data
about to whom they belong. (It takes years for the CDC to
generate birth stats, thus the lag in up-to-date information.)
Regardless of how planned the creation of the child was,
the bottom line is that the last time the number of annual
births was this high was way back in 1957 and 1961 (both
years saw 4.3 million births in the United States)[9] when
"overpopulation" was barely a concept to worry about, with
only a handful of people voicing their concern.

As I have shown in this book, for what you must go
through in order to adopt a child, upon completion, they
should confer upon you some degree like M.C.A., for *Master
of Child Adoption.* Adoption classes with a social worker,
mandatory books to read, background checks and so much
more are required before the governments of this and foreign
countries will allow a U.S. citizen to adopt a child. Why on
earth aren't there parent-licensing programs to make sure an
adult will be a good parent? Though I know this is a slippery
slope, and some people may equate my ideas with a kind of

population cleansing, I do believe that some discussion of limiting births is not unreasonable.

According to the website for Portland State University, an academic institution that hosts a Center for Sustainable Processes and Practices, "In a lifetime, the average American will throw away 600 times his or her adult weight in garbage. This means that each adult will leave a legacy of 90,000 lbs. of trash for his or her children." Multiply that amount by the more than four million people born each year in the United States of America, and you get more pounds of garbage than will appear in my calculator's window.

Where does all the garbage go? Landfills. During my research for this book, I tried to find somebody to provide me with statistics on how many landfills close and how many new ones are created each year. I started with the National Recycling Coalition in Washington, D.C., and spoke with the Director of Policies and Programs; he apologized, but had no data for me. Instead he directed me the U.S. Environmental Protection Agency (http://www.epa.gov/osw/nonhaz/municipal/pubs/msw07-rpt.pdf).

According to the EPA, as of 2008, there are 1,812 landfills in the U.S., excluding ten landfills in Hawaii and 300 in Alaska. The EPA also disclosed that there indeed have been landfills that have closed because they were filled to capacity. They do not, however, have specific information on landfill creations and closures because records are kept by individual states. I would not expect the EPA to endorse adoption as a way to reduce production of waste, even though it does stress that waste management should follow the hierarchy where the emphasis is on reducing, reusing, and recycling. As anybody living in this day and age would agree, the EPA believes that the least preferred method for waste disposal is landfilling, despite the profitability of this practice for those who own the land on which landfills are built. And, nobody wants some money-hungry landowner or municipal government approving a landfill in her or his backyard.

Thinking *there's always going to be someplace to make a dump* just isn't true. Overpopulation is a serious problem that mainstream media choose to ignore. Why isn't this subject taken seriously enough to show up on presidential and gubernatorial platforms? There is so much that can be done *now* to help slow the rate of population growth in the world. At www.overpopulation.org, a plethora of current overpopulation data is presented. The website's section called WOA!, or World Overpopulation Awareness, offers solid suggestions, including this: "The solutions seem simple: empower and enable women to have fewer children, develop simpler lifestyles, tax pollution of any kind, and set up government programs to enable the other three solutions."

Overpopulation has become an unfathomable planetary crisis. The uncomfortably named *Voluntary Human Extinction Movement*, located at http://www.vhemt.org, claims on its website: *Phasing out the human race by voluntarily ceasing to breed will allow Earth's biosphere to return to good health. Crowded conditions and resource shortages will improve as we become less dense.*

VHEMT spokesperson Les U. Knight states, "Adopting existing children avoids adding another wildlife habitat usurper to the excessive billions of us, provides parenting opportunities for couples who feel qualified, and gives life-saving care to children who would be languishing in miserable conditions. Until we eliminate the inhumane conditions which create orphans, an urgent, unfilled need for compassionate parents continues unabated. Adoption isn't a complete solution, it's simply the best we can do with a deplorable situation."

He further expressed, "My heart-felt congratulations and respect go out to adoptive parents who dedicate themselves to providing loving homes, nurturing children who otherwise have little opportunity for fulfilling lives."

Biological urges and needs are real. We all must eat, drink water, and sleep if we are to survive. Even sex is still considered a biological need in some circles. But, should insemination and procreation be considered a biological need? In this day and age, the human race must consider a wider arena, one that encompasses more than the self, if we are to survive.

I did not start writing this memoir as a forum to preach radical ideas to an audience that simply wanted to know about my journey of international adoption. But the more I realized how connected my beliefs about the environment and overpopulation were to my lean towards *not* procreating when I may have been physically able to, the more necessary it became to write about my statistical findings and beliefs with my readers. As a result of becoming so passionate about this subject and sharing my ideas with those who cross my path for whatever reasons, I realized, too, that I am not alone; I simply seem to be one of the few speaking her thoughts out loud.

It is my greatest hope that, just like when an overeater knows she must learn to override certain urges if she is to lose weight and become a healthy person, when a woman feels the urge to make another baby, she counts to ten, or ten-thousand, or ten-million, before she just goes ahead and does it. As controversial as this may sound to some of you, choosing not to give birth just might be the most important decision you ever make. For everyone.

APPENDIX B

INFERTILITY AND ITS
ROLE IN ADOPTION

*W*omen *sometimes go to great lengths to have children—witness [one] writer's recent tales of injecting herself with Italian nuns' urine and downing dubious herbal concoctions. The risks of pregnancy include a slightly higher chance of breast cancer for a time, and for women over 35, the higher odds may endure. Every woman has to decide for herself how to think about these risks.*

– http://www.slate.com/id/2163785

BY THE TIME A WOMAN reaches her forties, if she has not given birth, she most likely won't. What she may not know, however, is that the viability of her eggs began to diminish years before.

Once upon a time, it was common for a woman to start bearing children in her teens and twenties. If the onset of menstruation begins just after her first decade of life (which isn't necessarily the safest time to give birth), and the quantity and quality of her eggs diminish as she ages, the mathematics simply do not add up to make conception easy later in life.

During the 1950s, marriage and children were part of the national agenda. American media did its best to promote the need for a young woman to pursue a husband rather than a college degree. And it worked! Though she may have had other aspirations, if she was not engaged or married by her early twenties, she was surely on her way to becoming an "old maid." Staying home to be a homemaker was considered the appropriate way for a woman to be "successful" back then. Those who chose to work when they didn't need the paycheck were likely labeled "selfish."[10]

The following data help illustrate why today's couples are having trouble getting pregnant and delivering a healthy child without the use of artificial intervention. In 1900, 5.1 million women worked outside the home. Recent information gathered found that by 2007, this number had increased to 67.8 million. By 2014, projections estimate that the number of working women will reach almost 76 million.[11]

Delaying the age at which a woman attempts to conceive, because she instead enters the workforce, ultimately makes getting pregnant when she finally wants to quite a difficult endeavor. In addition to fewer viable eggs, there is an increased chance of endometriosis. By the time a woman becomes peri-menopausal (beginning from age 35 to age 45, depending on family history and individual constitution), there can be a 50 percent chance that she has developed endometriosis, a condition that at least 25 percent, and up to 50 percent, of infertile women harbor. Endometriosis develops only during the time when a woman has her menstrual cycle, and is "common in women who have had uninterrupted cyclic menstruation for periods of more than five years," which means "a woman who has had a period every month for five years [that] has not been interrupted by pregnancy."[12] Though sometimes there are no accompanying symptoms, often the pain and discomfort that signifies something is not right sends the woman to her physician to find out what is wrong. If the woman is trying to get pregnant, she may end up discovering the culprit of her infertility.

Without exploratory surgery, however, it is not possible to know without a shadow of doubt that endometriosis is the reason she is not able to conceive or carry a pregnancy to term.

Though it is true that infertility has become a huge problem for couples desiring to have children today, it is also true that they no longer need to suffer in silence. It is possible now to seek and find the comfort of a community. On October 16, 2010, in conjunction with National Infertility Awareness Week, a Fertility Expo took place in San Diego that was presented and sponsored by Reproductive Wellness, a clinic that specializes in acupuncture and integrative medicine for infertility. Other sponsors included fertility clinics and doctors. A nutritionist as well as the Adoption Alliance participated. It is clear that alternatives and support do exist for those wishing to explore all options before immediately opting for infertility drug therapy.

WHEN PLANS GO AWRY—OR—HOW *CLOMID* GAINED ITS FAME

Even before the idea of giving a sibling to their first child came about, it was obvious that forty-five-year-old Holly and her forty-plus husband would have a challenge building a family with their genetic material. Holly had two miscarriages before giving birth to their son, who is now three. She and her husband had decided they would wait awhile to have their second child; an eighteen-month wait would have been their ideal. Then, with two birth children, the plan was to adopt. But, even though they did have that one successful pregnancy a few years back, it was not as simple the second time around.

One year after the birth of their son, they started trying again. No luck. But when he was about eighteen months old, Holly did become pregnant. Soon, however, she lost the fetus. Six months later, they tried again. Nothing. By April 2007, about a year after they started trying to get pregnant again, they met with a nurse practitioner who specialized in infertility. They spent the summer experimenting with her suggestions without any luck. By August 2007, they started to feel desperate and decided to try clomiphene citrate (Clomid), a fertility drug that works in the hypothalamus and is prescribed to women to help cultivate eggs and mature follicles in their ovaries.

Holly admits that when she and her husband decided she should try the drug, it opened a can of fertility worms. "That started us on the god-awful infertility treadmill," she says, where hopes rise and hopes are dashed. One seemingly simple step like swallowing a pill can easily carry a woman to the next more invasive step. The momentum just keeps building and sucks you into a world that you never knew existed. The idea of a happy outcome is so enticing that the pressure to try more and more invasive treatments in order to get pregnant becomes nearly impossible to pass up.

The first month, Holly took the full dose of Clomid. (Many physicians advocate taking the drug for only three months at a time.) The pain, she says, was unbearable because too many eggs developed. She could not stand up without agonizing discomfort in her abdomen. She knew that the likelihood of ending up with multiple births was high if they went forward with fertilization, so she and her husband did nothing to pursue a pregnancy during this first round. "I couldn't reduce, as they say." Holly knew she did not have it in her to terminate any of the potential fetuses, and it is possible there would have been many.

The second month Holly took a half dose of Clomid, then had a shot of progesterone in order for the eggs to release. Intercourse becomes quite clinical now, needing to be timed nearly to the minute. "You know," she recalls, "it's not fun." Even though they had done everything exactly as they were told, she did not get pregnant. Or maybe she did, but lost it, because this menstrual cycle was different, more painful than usual, and afterwards she became sick.

The third and last attempt with Clomid took place a few months later. They were paying out of pocket for these expensive treatments, and her husband had just quit his job. She explains that during this time her thoughts went something like this: "I can't keep doing this, we don't have the money, I don't have the emotional stamina." This would be the last try. They went through the scenario again and headed to the doctor's office to have blood drawn. The expedited results arrived that afternoon over the telephone. Not pregnant.

"I collapsed in a heap on the floor and bawled," she recalls. By now, they were getting quite desperate, as anyone could imagine. The spiral was spinning out of control, and it was their practitioner who had to remind them that upon their initial meeting Holly and her husband had voiced clearly that they did not want to use invasive treatments. So when Holly requested going further, the practitioner did not support it. Had they not had such a conscientious advocate, the next step would have been to take another round of Clomid, but this time instead of being inseminated through intercourse, they would have taken washed sperm and inserted them through the cervix directly into the uterus with a catheter, a procedure known as Intra-Uterine Insemination (IUI). The reason for trying it this way is that the delicate sperm have less distance to travel, bypassing the cervix and being deposited straight into the uterus.

Though Holly's husband supported them continuing to try to get pregnant via artificial means, she had had enough. "There was a lot of grieving," she remembers. Today, a year later, the grief has not disappeared.

Like many infertile women, Holly questioned the "spiritual reasons" for her inability to carry a pregnancy to term again. "Am I not a good enough person?" Some infertile couples would not empathize with Holly's plight because she has one birth child whom she gets to parent. But she disagrees. "It's almost worse because you don't understand why it doesn't work when it worked before."

Adding insult to injury, before Holly's husband was able to find another well-paying job, she was denied health insurance by Blue Cross and Presbyterian. Why? The Clomid. It seems that these very large insurance companies put women on a three-year probation after receiving infertility drugs. Why would the decision-makers at *Big Insurance Co., Inc.* find women who previously took Clomid to be uninsurable?

"THE LURKING ELIZABETH EDWARDS QUESTION: **Do Pregnancy and Fertility Treatment Increase the Risk of Breast Cancer?**" read a headline posted on April 9, 2007, on the website www.slate.com.

Elizabeth Edwards gave birth to her then-husband John's son on July 18, 1979. In a tragic car accident on April 4, 1996, the seventeen-year-old died, leaving the grieving couple with their only other child, a daughter, three years his junior.

Fast forward some sixteen years after their second child was born. Elizabeth Edwards is now in her forties, and lo and behold, she gives birth to another girl, followed two years later with the birth of their son. By 2008 it is common web knowledge that Elizabeth Edwards underwent assisted reproduction therapy in order to build this latter part of her family with John. Sadly, she was diagnosed with breast cancer in 2004 and passed away in December 2010.

Back in May 2006 a study revealed an inconclusive link between the general use of infertility drugs and breast cancer, but did show that infertile women who were specifically treated with Clomid had an elevated risk for developing breast cancer. This study was conducted on Israeli women and not widely distributed.

Not until April 15, 2008, did a definitive study, carried out at the Comprehensive Breast Care Institute, Assaf Harofeh Medical Center at the Tel-Aviv University in Israel, conclude that, "A possible association between IVF therapy and breast cancer development was demonstrated, especially in women >or=40 years of age" (*Annals of Surgical Oncology*).

IN 2003, AFTER FIVE YEARS of infertility treatments, Leslie, an attorney living in Washington, D.C., gave birth to a healthy baby girl. About two years after her daughter was born, Leslie developed breast cancer. Now she believes that the fertility drugs she took to become pregnant may have caused or contributed to her cancer. She even began researching whether she might be able to bring a lawsuit against the pharmaceutical companies on behalf of a class of women who underwent fertility treatment and later developed breast cancer.

Leslie's intense desire to experience pregnancy, childbirth, and breastfeeding came in part from her mother, who in the late 1950s and early 1960s had researched natural childbirth and had given birth to two healthy children without the use of numbing drugs. While conducting interviews for this book with women who had given birth, and with those who still wanted to, I could feel the intense desire many women have to become a mommy. Beyond a longing to become a parent and raise a child, these women yearn to experience any or all of the biological aspects of having a baby, including the physical changes during pregnancy, labor and delivery, and breast-feeding.

During my interview with Leslie she shared that her mother had to change obstetricians several times in order to find a doctor who would even consider delivering her babies naturally. While in college, Leslie further researched the neurology of endorphins that the body releases during childbirth. She felt passionate about experiencing this herself. Though I have been reluctant to admit that I had off and on felt this desire, in part I am sure because I did not marry at an age where getting pregnant would be a more natural choice, I can admit that the urge to experience the physical aspects of bio-motherhood was real; I just wouldn't allow myself to go there because I did not have a willing partner.

Leslie did marry early, though, and when she and her husband failed to get pregnant, pursuing adoption as a means to parenthood felt like a loss. Her longing was not about passing on her genetics, which for some adults is their main impetus to have children. What Leslie felt she would miss was the actual physical aspects of motherhood. Thus she spent half a decade using artificial means to get pregnant. In the end, the drugs worked. But not, she believes, without possibly leading her to develop cancer.

"I believe that there is a causal connection and no one talks about this—certainly not to the millions of women who undergo fertility treatments in this country every year. I would have still done it, but I would have done it differently, being much more careful to limit the number of stimulation cycles I put my body through. And I would have worked with a different doctor—the one I ultimately got pregnant working with. There are a lot of quacks out there who will stimulate over and over again, month after month. And they don't even monitor hormone levels. It's really a crime.

"I'm convinced that in about twenty years—if not sooner—we will see a huge rise in breast cancer linked to fertility hormone treatments. All the women who sat in the IVF clinic with me will now be sitting in the Clinical Cancer

Center. I'm certain in ten or twenty years [though], as my cohort of women who underwent fertility treatments reach our fifties and sixties, it will start coming out. Just as it did with post-menopausal hormone replacement treatment. It's pretty obvious: if you shoot yourself up with estrogen, your body is likely to rebel."

Still, Leslie understands a woman's desire to experience pregnancy, birthing a child, and breast feeding. She encourages all women who feel the kind of passion she felt to research what they are getting into before beginning fertility treatments to facilitate their pregnancies. There are things a woman can do to help her know if she is a likely breast cancer candidate. That way, she can make a more informed choice about the level of risk she is taking.

Leslie recommends that women, before undergoing fertility treatments, check out certain things: "Determine whether you have the genetic mutations on the BRCA 1 or 2 genes that are correlated with breast cancer, get the very best fertility doctor/clinic available and ensure s/he/they are using the most up to date methods, and [that they] limit the number of stimulation cycles to which you subject your body.

"I definitely think women—and men—should consider adoption. But I also understand deeply the desire some women—and men—have to become pregnant and give birth to a child they will parent. It is complicated. If we knew with certainty that undergoing fertility treatments would lead us to develop breast or other cancer, I doubt many of us would do it. But because nothing in life is definitely going to happen at a specific time, we gamble and weigh the risks and benefits."

If a woman thoughtfully decides she is not willing to risk the possibility of developing cancer in order to get pregnant, then the loss of bio-motherhood won't hurt as much. Adoption, then, will seem like the perfect option for growing her family.

THE CHALLENGES OF INTERNATIONAL ADOPTION & THE SECRET LIFE OF AN INFERTILE COUPLE

On a clear summer day in Taos, New Mexico, 2008, Pamela leads me into a conference room inside the plush offices of her downtown real estate building. She shuts the door behind her, asks me to choose wherever I would like to sit around the large, mahogany table. Business is not so good these days, houses are not selling; she has some time and is eager to share her story.

Ten years ago, Pamela and her husband Robert were in their early forties. Before trying infertility drugs, they had used numerous alternative means to become pregnant, including Chinese acupuncture, herbs, and bodywork. Initially, drugs were their last resort. The couple promised themselves they would never resort to IVF. "That was a no-fly zone," she admits.

During one of Pamela's ovulation cycles, her father had a heart attack. She immediately flew to Texas, without her husband—he had to work. No time for remorse that she was missing a precious opportunity to be impregnated; this was Pamela's father.

One afternoon, while she was staying at her brother's house during her father's recuperation, the phone rang and she picked it up. One of her brother's childhood friends was on the other end. They started talking and the friend shared with Pamela that he and his wife had recently adopted a child from Vietnam. Pamela responded in a way that most people do when they find out that somebody has chosen to adopt, especially internationally.

"Oh, that's so nice of you," she recalls saying.

The friend, however, surprised Pamela with his reply. He denied that he was the nice one. "She's changed my life," he told her, speaking of his adopted daughter. "I am so grateful to her!"

Six months later, Pamela was exhausted with the infertility treatments—on every level. One morning she woke up and told Robert, "That's it. We're adopting. We're adopting from Vietnam."

Though Pamela felt "a little like a failure," the process started out smoothly, which helped. "It was so easy," she recalls now. The wife of her brother's friend worked at an agency that adopted from Vietnam, so she hired her. Four months after submitting their paperwork, they had a referral.

She returned home from work one afternoon to find *the* envelope waiting for her in the mail. (This was back when email was not an everyday means of communication. Now, nearly all adoption correspondence is transmitted via email.)

"I was scared, but I was excited." Hours and hours passed as Pamela went about her evening chores with the envelope staring her down from the dining room table. Her husband was away on business so it wasn't as if she was waiting for him to come home. "That was my little girl in that envelope," she recalls with a sparkle in her eyes. Finally, she opened the envelope from which she pulled out the child referral form and a photograph. "It was instant," she remembers, recalling the immediate bond she felt with the image on the photograph.

Her reaction upon seeing the photograph strikes me as similar to what so many couples feel the first time they see the ultrasound image of their unborn baby. Even though there is still much that can go wrong, in a pregnancy and for that matter in an adoption, the very strong emotional bonds begin to develop.

From then on, Pamela says, "It was agonizing. It's a wrenching process."

Starting out on the road to adoption is a little like discovering you are pregnant, in that there is an initial excitement about the *idea* of becoming a mother. As the weeks and months play out, however, the so-called adoption "morning sickness" sets in. Analogous to being pregnant, waiting through every tedious step of the adoption process can at times be quite painful. Especially when it comes to international adoption, with the myriad of individual governmental regulations, holidays, customs, and cultural standards that are inherent within each country. Often when prospective parents choose a country from which to adopt a child, they do not consider what setbacks they might encounter. Having interviewed many parents who went through international adoption, as well as having experienced the process myself, I can honestly say that becoming more educated about the country from which you wish to adopt should be a vital part of the pre-adoption process. Too often, the roadblocks that are encountered are not expected, and thus cause unnecessary stress.

This was the case with Pamela and Robert, who were not prepared to put their adoption on hold until Tet, the Vietnamese New Year, was over. Further, once they were able to go to Vietnam and bring their nine-month-old daughter home, Pamela admitted, "the stress did not end."

Many prospective parents, perhaps, in fact, *most* first-time parents—biological, step, or adoptive—cannot fathom the change that will take place once a baby enters the scene. If a parent is not mentally prepared, the change can be totally overwhelming. What Pamela may not have realized is that the chaos she experienced as a newly adoptive mother is like any new mother experiencing the non-stop needs that a baby brings with her or him.

In the end, though, Pamela and Robert got what they had endlessly longed for: a family. "The whole concept of family feels so good," she says. "Suddenly holidays, vacations, celebrations, all have more meaning."

Ten years later, Pamela expresses what most adoptive parents I have spoken to tell me. "There is no difference. My daughter is my daughter, and I cannot imagine loving her any more than I do. It makes no difference whatsoever that I did not give birth to her."

FROM THE PAGES OF WWW.RESOLVE.ORG (The National Infertility Association):

> *Infertility can be a major life crisis. The infertility experience involves many hidden losses for individuals, their loved ones, and society as a whole, including:*
>
> * *Loss of the pregnancy and birth experience*

- *Loss of a genetic legacy*
- *Loss of the parenting experience*
- *Loss of a grandparenting relationship*
- *Loss of feelings of self-worth*
- *Loss of stability in family and personal relationships*
- *Loss of work productivity*
- *Loss of a sense of spirituality and sense of hope for the future*

Because infertility often involves major personal life issues and decisions, it is often experienced as a private matter, and is not ordinarily discussed in public forums. The personal nature of the infertility experience contributes to the failure of society to recognize infertility as a disease thus creating a lack of sound knowledge about infertility.

Infertility has a strong impact on self-esteem. Suddenly your life, which may have been well planned and successful, seems out of control. Not only is the physical body not responding as expected but it feels as if your entire life is on hold. Facing the disappointment of not becoming pregnant month after month can lead to depression. Studies have shown that infertility depression levels can rival those of cancer.

PERHAPS NOBODY KNOWS THE GRIEF of infertility better than Sharon, a forty-three-year-old woman living in northern New Mexico with her husband and newly adopted Ethiopian toddlers. Today, she admits that she's still not "completely over it." She continues to ask herself, "Did we try everything we could have?"

Newly wed at age thirty-five, Sharon and her husband Rick were eager to start a family. Though she knew she had a uterine fibroid, because it was not causing her pain she never really thought it would pose an obstacle to getting pregnant. During an exam to help discover why she was not getting pregnant, Dr. Morrow suggested she undergo an invasive procedure to have the fibroid removed. She wasn't ready to be cut open, so she and Rick sought a second opinion. Dr. McNabb, a University Hospital physician, was on a slower track, and suggested she try Intra-Uterine Insemination, the procedure that Holly used.

Over a six-month period, the suggested maximum length of time to ingest Clomid, Sharon was artificially inseminated four times. This method, Sharon explained, is a relatively inexpensive process compared to other methods. Unfortunately, she did not get pregnant. Dr. McNabb's next step was to try to remove the potentially inhibiting fibroid with dilation and curettage, a procedure called a D&C. This procedure involves expanding the opening of the uterus enough for a thin, sharp tool to curettage or suction away the lining of the uterus. In Sharon's case, the fibroid would be scraped away, with the idea of removing extrauterine tissue that might be crowding out healthy organs that would normally allow a pregnancy to occur. After three unsuccessful D&C procedures, this doctor too believed that the course of treatment should be a traditional surgery to remove the fibroid. At that time, she again refused the scalpel.

Denver-based Dr. Link, who is a partner at Dr. Morrow's practice, encouraged Sharon and Rick to next try IVF. This doctor, whose website boasts, "Over the past 7 years, we have helped couples create over 600 babies and we would like to help you create the family you desire," insisted that Sharon sign a contract stating that she and her husband would try IVF four times, at a cost of $30,000, not including the drugs she would have to take to prepare her body for implantation. They agreed, and moved into a friend's house outside Denver for two weeks in order to use this doctor.

IVF is not as simple as it sounds: collecting the eggs and the sperm, fertilizing them in a Petri dish, and inserting the mixture directly into the uterus. A woman's body needs to be ready to receive the baby-making concoction, which involves much more than people imagine.

"People don't even know what [IVF] entails," Sharon says. "I was injecting myself in parking lots." At a party once, Sharon and Rick retreated to the bathroom so they could "shoot up" in private with the two-inch IM (intramuscular) needle filled with the necessary hormones.

"It was really hard. I was doing acupuncture two times a week, working fulltime, taking a lot of drugs, driving hours and hours to doctor appointments. I pretty much went ballistically crazy. I don't know how I survived, really."

After the first failed IVF treatment, Sharon took a "Clomid Challenge Test," which she claims should have been performed prior to being inseminated. Because after she failed the test, Dr. Link reneged on his end of the contract, now insisting that instead of completing four rounds of IVF, she try a donor egg.

Rather than complete their pregnancy attempts with this doctor, who they felt had manipulated them into giving him a huge amount of money, Sharon and Rick decided to return to Dr. Morrow. By now, Sharon was desperate enough to put herself through the invasive surgery that would remove the supposedly pregnancy-preventing fibroid. A few months later, after a second failed IVF treatment, at a cost of $15,000, Dr. Morrow also suggested they use a donor egg. Sharon and her husband dejectedly agreed.

During the preliminary search for a suitable donor Sharon perused the photographs and profiles of young, fertile women. This last-resort process revolted her. She felt envious of these women, and angry, defeated and deflated. "Oh my God," she remembers thinking, "this is so surreal."

In addition to feeling ridiculous about how far she had gone to get pregnant, Sharon began to feel disgusted with the infertility industry. "I got this real sour taste for doctors," she admits now, explaining her beliefs about the fertility specialists who dismiss unsuccessful women from their practice because it's bad for business. Why else wouldn't Dr. Link complete his contract that committed to four IVF treatments? Why else would Dr. Morrow encourage a donor egg rather than trying a few more rounds of IVF? Each failed attempt to get a woman pregnant lowers the clinic's success statistics, thereby eliminating the desire to publish current data on a website.

Finally, after more than $50,000, and incalculable emotional stress, Rick said, "Let's just adopt."

At first they wanted to try an infant adoption, wherein a couple hires a private attorney to find a pregnant woman who wants to give up her baby for adoption, and then facilitates the transaction. But Sharon confessed that she did not want to have to convince a bio-mom that she and her husband would be the right adoptive parents. Many of the birth mothers seeking to give up their child for adoption, Sharon explained, are young and addicted to drugs. "I could not sell myself to a drug mom who doesn't deserve it anyway," she said, obviously bitter with her own loss of fertility. "I have a real problem with that."

Years ago, Sharon had taught at an international school in Zambia for eighteen months. She has an affinity for the people of Africa, and since her husband was not interested in Asia, and since most African countries insist that adoptive families live with their new child in the country for up to two years, they decided on Ethiopia, where adoptions, at the time that they were pursuing this idea, could be finalized inside the country within a week.

Sharon has had her children home with her for over six months now. And though she adores her boys and appreciates the joys of motherhood, she cannot shake the notion that she still has a uterus and, at least in her mind, it is still possible for her to give birth. During our lengthy conversation, I told Sharon about my hysterectomy, and that adoption was a no-brainer for my husband and me because any other means of becoming parents (aside from surrogacy, which we never considered) was surgically removed from our options. When Sharon learned that I no longer had a uterus, she admitted that she has often thought how much easier it would be on her psyche if she would simply have hers removed through an elective hysterectomy. That way, her mind would never be tempted to fantasize about the possibility of getting pregnant.

Now Sharon feels isolated and angry, uncomfortable engaging in the "normal" rituals of friends' pregnancies.

She feels resentful and annoyed at the seeming callousness of those who know she was unable to give birth. She has, in fact, hosted five baby showers over the last several years. In the middle of a recent preparation for a baby shower, she chose to bow out.

"People who are fertile don't have any idea how bad it is. I can't even talk to people in the fertile world because they have no clue. I've had two years of therapy, and I could use five more. Sharon believes that society views infertility as a choice. "As if it's my fault," she says, "because I waited too long."

NICOLE LIVES IN LOS ANGELES and co-owns with her husband an art gallery in Santa Monica. Her story, though similar in some ways to the other women described in this chapter, ended with a positive emotional response to her eventual adoption.

Married at age twenty-eight to a man twenty years her senior, John, Nicole failed to get pregnant naturally, even though they were trying since their 1997 wedding. By 2001, the couple was frustrated enough to pursue treatments with a fertility specialist. During a natural ovulation cycle, her husband's sperm was artificially inseminated into her uterus. As fate had it, she became pregnant on the first insemination. Twelve weeks later, the fetus died *in utero*. Though grief stricken, Nicole and John figured that if it was that easy to get pregnant, albeit through artificial insemination, they might as well try again. Nine tries and eighteen months later, they gave up.

This time, Nicole's grief overwhelmed her. She sought therapy, cried a lot, and tried to keep an open mind to other options. Adoption, though, was "unfathomable."

One afternoon, she returned home from work with a phone message from her mother, an optimistic New Jersey transplant who had given birth to three children. Nicole's mother is also grandmother to four biological grandchildren; she knows first hand the joys of parenting and wanted to encourage her daughter to do whatever it took in order for her to become a mother.

"'You adopted your kittens,' Mom said, 'so you can adopt a baby.'"

Her mother was a smart woman; anyone who has gone through an animal adoption, especially a woman who has never parented a child, can relate to the experience of adoption. We who have loved and cared for our animals as if they were our children know first hand that it does not take long to fall in love with a rescued animal and feel as if it's been a part of your family forever.

"I really had to do a lot of soul-searching," Nicole now admits.

"[Becoming a parent] was a great need in *me*," she recalls, reflecting on how she had once viewed adoption only as a way to "save the children." Although she didn't convey any strong bio-motherhood urges, she grew to see that adoption was also a way to "save" a person who can't get pregnant.

"I'd always loved Asian things. Why not love an Asian baby?"

When I asked Nicole if she had considered other programs, easier perhaps as far as length of stay in the country, or even a domestic adoption, she expressed the need she had to immerse herself in her future daughter's culture. "I wanted to go to China, to live there, be in her birth place. I wanted the whole cultural experience of an international adoption; I wanted to labor."

When Nicole speaks about her experience of traveling to China with her husband to bring home their daughter, her eyes glow. When asked if she has any advice for women and men dealing with infertility issues, she tells me that she wishes she had never even gone for that first insemination. Her daughter is the light and love of her life. She feels that it was a waste to put herself through so much physical and emotional trauma knowing now how gratifying and even natural being a mother to her adopted daughter is.

"Infertility treatment is so difficult," she shares. "I hope I can spare someone the grief and pain of, *Can I?* and *What if?* There are other ways to be a mother. There are so many beautiful children all over the world. If your desire is so big to be a parent, keep your heart open to other options."

Nicole knows from the most personal, direct experience what can happen when you stay openhearted and ready to receive the love you seek. Just one look at her as she holds her beautiful daughter, and everybody else does too.

THROUGH THE VARIOUS EXAMPLES PRESENTED in this appendix, it is clear that there are many reasons why we want to become a parent, and various ways to do so. Leslie's strong desire to experience bio-motherhood dictated her self-admitted haste, and even perhaps neglect, in choosing the type and length of her fertility treatments. Though her path did indeed lead to a successful pregnancy and the birth of a healthy child, she would not do it the same way again. Even though she became a bio-mom, she also battled breast cancer and is now hoping to shed light on an industry that she believes undervalues women's long-term health.

If a woman has the financial resources and emotional stamina to endure the roller coaster of infertility treatments, and she is totally committed to doing whatever it takes to become a bio-mom, including the possibility of risking cancer, then of course she (and her partner) should go for it. However, I think that it is vital for women to objectively consider the various means available and to investigate as many stories as possible. We all have to realize that no matter how much time, money, tears, and anxiety we spend, sometimes we just don't get what we want.

As illustrated in this appendix, many women who undergo fertility treatments do not get pregnant. With this in mind, perhaps some people can draw great inspiration from Nicole's story. Had she known how fulfilling her experience of adopting her daughter would be, Nicole admits that she would not have spent one penny or one minute on infertility treatments. She cannot imagine feeling any more love or connection to her adoptive daughter than if she had given birth to her. So even though there are aspects of bio-motherhood that adoptive motherhood can never satisfy, when people focus on parenting a child, rather than the nine-month process of becoming a mother, they *will* find great joy in being an adoptive parent.

THE HISTORY OF AND HOW TO BEGIN AN ADOPTION

With the advent of the industrial revolution in the mid-1800s, increased urbanization brought with it big city problems that initiated the opening of orphanages in the United States. "By 1850, New York state had 27 orphanages run by both public and private funds and yet there was still an estimated 10,000 street kids with no home or guardian."[13]

In 1851, the state of Massachusetts passed the *Adoption of Children Act*, considered the first adoption law, which "recogniz[ed] adoption as a social and legal operation based on child welfare rather than adult interests." The Act is considered historically relevant because it gave judges the authority to decree whether or not an adoption was "fit and proper."[14]

Approximately 620,000 men died during the Civil War, which took place from 1861 to 1865, and further contributed to the country's orphan count. While the streets grew far too populated with children, this was also the time in our country when institutions like prisons, insane asylums, and orphanages began to appear. Between 1910 and 1930, the first specialized adoption agencies were founded, creating a philanthropic way to offer a solution "for illegitimate children, unmarried mothers, and infertile couples."[15] However, by the 1950s and '60s, attitudes towards childcare slowly started to change. "Society believed that children do better in a family environment and gradually the closures of orphanages in the 1960-1975 period gave rise to foster care and group homes all over North America."[16]

Today, having replaced orphanages, foster care is the most common way in which couples obtain domestically adopted children. Foster care is used as a social welfare option for at-risk children who are being neglected or abused at home. According to a June 5, 2007, report written by Dan Lips, Senior Policy Analyst at the Heritage Foundation, the approximately "518,000 American children currently in foster care are among the most at-risk children in American society." Many foster children will live in numerous homes and go to many different schools by the time they reach adulthood. This unstable lifestyle accounts for why so many of these children end up homeless, in jail, or reliant on state services.

According to Jill May, Foster Care and Adoption Bureau Chief with New Mexico Children, Youth and Families Department (CYFD), "Adopting out of foster care does not have to be as daunting as its reputation has made it seem." However, Ms. May stressed that prospective adoptive parents should obtain as much information about the foster child's history as possible. It appears that the possibility of an adopted foster child being returned to the foster care system increases when the adopted parents just don't know enough about the child's past to make an informed decision about whether or not they will be able to meet that child's future needs. Of course, many prospective parents are unaware of the difficulties associated with raising any child, especially one in foster care who may have a variety of emotional problems. It is important for the future parents to take a thorough inventory of their personal resources and honestly evaluate any limitations they may have before adopting such a child.

In further support of foster adoption, the Heritage Foundation Report also stated that in 2006 Arizona's Governor Janet Napolitano "signed the nation's first K-12 scholarship program for foster kids." The following year saw at least four states introduce similar legislation.[17] Further indications that foster reform is edging closer to reality came when President Bush signed into law on October 7, 2008, the "Fostering Connections to Success and Increasing Adoptions Act of 2008 (HR 6893)" (see: http://www.nacac.org/).

Under the Obama administration the horizon looks better than ever, as government assistance for foster care may be coming. Barack Obama's 2008 candidacy platform stated, "The foster care system is failing children who need help the most." Because this administration recognizes that the system is struggling, one goal they have is to provide support. Both President Obama and Vice President Biden believe that better training for foster parents and more foster homes are keys to helping this broken system. They hope to be able to restructure how law enforcement and child welfare officials communicate so that abuse within this system can come to an end.

With much needed improvement to the foster care system we will have the opportunity to step up and help children in our own country. It is exciting for me to think about the future possibilities for adoptive parents. Until these changes occur, however, it takes courageous and selfless people to choose to adopt a foster child. Some day, and this day is coming, choosing to adopt a foster child may just be a first choice to grow a family.

For both a domestic and an international adoption, a home study is mandatory. Though the requirements vary from state to state, generally you will have to submit an initial form to an adoption social worker. You will be interviewed and evaluated, and eventually deemed qualified or not to adopt according to your state's guidelines. Background checks, financial reviews, and at least one home visit are usually required. During the home study process, each adoptive parent-to-be learns about the adoption process and about parenting an adopted child.

Though completing a home study often feels redundant and at times even silly, the process is not just to protect the child from potentially dangerous parents. The home study is also important for the prospective parents, in that it gives them an opportunity to decide if they really and truly want to go through with adopting.

The home study is just the beginning of the long journey you will take to adopt your child. Had Brian and I known in advance about all that the home study entailed, our entire process would have gone more smoothly. I highly recommend starting your home study prior to deciding from where you want to adopt. During the hours of training, vital information about all aspects of adoption is presented that can help you make what will soon be life-altering decisions. Without a pre-determined agenda, you may discover that a domestic foster adoption is for you, or that you actually do want to parent a child from infancy, even if you'll have to deal with diapers and bottles and such. Going through the home study *first* will help inform the decisions you eventually make.

In addition, with a completed home study, you are eligible to join the Rainbow Kids database (www.rainbowkids.com), which provides you with a major advantage: you can review waiting children that are available for adoption. These kids are placed with a variety of accredited adoption agencies, which makes it even smarter to choose your agency *after* completing a home study.

My husband and I, however, put the cart before the horse. We did not actually find our social worker until *after* we had decided on an agency and a country from where we wanted to adopt. I do not recommend this sequence. If I had to do it over again, I would have started by consulting the *National Foster Care & Adoption Directory* (http://www. childwelfare.gov/nfcad), a searchable database that lists public and licensed private agencies. Having started our adoption process somewhat backwards, my best advice for those who are even slightly unsure from where they want to adopt is that you begin by hiring a qualified adoption social worker to conduct your home study.

When your home study is complete, you will have a better idea of how you want to proceed with your adoption. Then, and only then, should you pursue a particular country from where you wish to adopt your child. In this systematic way, you will come to know yourself and your partner in a way that will help you feel good about the forever decision you are about to make.

ENDNOTES

BODY OF BOOK:

1. For more on Zen Buddhism and Master Deshimaru, see: http://www.zen-azi.org

2. On December 12, 2007, Assistant Secretary of State for Consular Affairs Maura Harty formalized the United States' ratification of the Hague Convention on Intercountry Adoption at a ceremony at The Hague, and our country became a full member on April 1, 2008.

3. The name of the agency that we hired for our adoption, in addition to the names of all of the agency's employees, has been changed.

4. http://www.sacred-destinations.com/ethiopia/addis-ababa-lucy.htm

5. http://www.unicef.org/infobycountry/ethiopia_30783.html

6. Margot Sunderland, The Science of Parenting (New York, NY: D.K. Publishing, Inc., 2008).

APPENDIX A:

7. http://womenshistory.about.com/od/abortionuslegal/p/roe_v_wade.htm

8. http://www.sustainer.org; Donella H. Meadows, Adjunct Professor of Environmental Studies at Dartmouth College.

9. http://geography.about.com/od/populationgeography/a/babyboom.htm

APPENDIX B:

10. This information can be found on the PBS website. See: www.pbs.org/wgbh/amex/pill/peopleevents/p_mrs.html

11. http://www.dpeaflcio.org/programs/factsheets/fs_2008_Professional_Women.htm

12. http://www.bioscience.org

APPENDIX C:

13. http://www.legends.ca/orphanages/orphanHistory.html

14. http://www.uoregon.edu/~adoption/timeline.html

15. Ibid.

16. http://www.legends.ca/orphanages/orphanHistory.html

17. http://www.heritage.org/research/education/bg2039.cfm

RESOURCES

http://www.adoption.state.gov/ This website is a must for all embarking on, and going through, the process of an international adoption.

http://adoption.state.gov/parents.html Please visit this site and click on: **The Hague Convention on Intercountry Adoption: A Guide for Prospective Parents.** This is a must-read for all prospective international adoptive parents.

http://adoption.state.gov/news/ethiopia.html Follow this site to keep up-to-date on the continuing news, changes in policy, and discussion about international adoption from Ethiopia.

http://wwwnc.cdc.gov/travel/content/vaccinations.aspx Check here for up-to-date information about what vaccines the government recommends for traveling abroad.

http://www.fistulacare.org/pages/index.php for more information about obstetric fistulas and how you can help.

http://www.amharickids.com A great website for purchasing meaningful and educational books and fair trade handicrafts for your Ethiopian child, and her/his adoptive family.

http://www.adoptiontribepublishing.com Founded by Michelle Madrid-Branch, author of *The Tummy Mummy* and *Adoption Means Love: Triumph of the Heart.*

http://www.inacookattorney.com Ina Cook, an adoption attorney and an adoptive mother, is dedicated to helping families find the adoption process that is right for them and will guide them from beginning to end of the adoption process.

http://camptobelong.org Founded by Lynn Price (www.lynnprice.com), a national award winner and author of *Real Belonging, Give Siblings Their Right to Reunite.* Camp To Belong is a non-profit organization dedicated to reuniting siblings placed in separate foster homes or other out-of-home care.

http://www.tapestrybooks.com An online bookstore specializing in a wide range of books on adoption.

http://www.ahopeforchildren.org AHOPE for Children is a non-profit organization whose mission is to serve the children of Ethiopia, with a primary emphasis on caring for orphans infected with HIV.

http://www.thereisnomewithoutyou.com A website that supports award-winning writer Melissa Fay Greene and her acclaimed book, *There Is No Me Without You*. This site is a great resource for prospective and current parents of Ethiopian children.

PHOTOS

Dina and Aster together for the first time.

Brian and Aster in Addis Ababa.

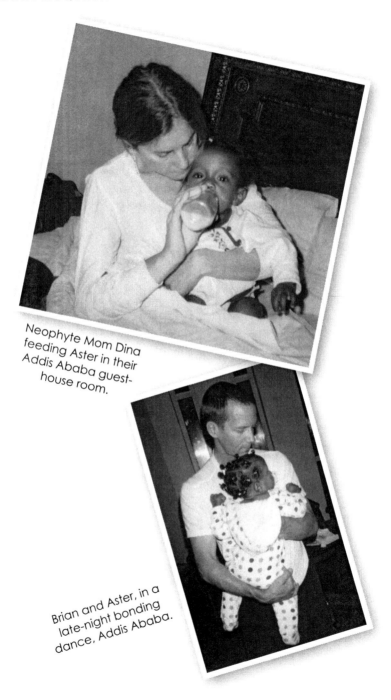

Neophyte Mom Dina feeding Aster in their Addis Ababa guest-house room.

Brian and Aster, in a late-night bonding dance, Addis Ababa.

Happy Baby Aster playing with Daddy's hat, Addis Ababa.

December 2009.

Family Photo, Thanksgiving 2010.

ABOUT THE AUTHOR

In 1998 Dina received her master's degree in Biography/Autobiography from Vermont's Goddard College. Prior to Dina's graduate study research, she came upon her grandfather Robert J. Wolff's manuscript, *The Man From Highbelow*. Fascinated with his story of awakening as an artist, and the way that through discovering his life she better understood  and accepted who she was, Dina decided to dedicate her life to facilitating the writing of memoir. Since then, she has helped dozens of writers discover the story they want to tell, and helped them write and publish their memoirs. Dina is the 2006 New Mexico Discovery Award winner in the category of Fiction. She lives in Santa Fe, New Mexico, with her husband, Brian, and daughter, Aster. Please visit www.FindingAster.com to engage with her about her life as an adoptive mother and other adoption-related topics.

LaVergne, TN USA
27 February 2011
218093LV00002B/4/P

9 781592 995134